VICTORIA & ALBERT MUSEUM

The Kashmir Shawl

JOHN IRWIN

LONDON

HER MAJESTY'S STATIONERY OFFICE

1973

ISBN 0 11 290164 6

CONTENTS

ACKNOWLEDGEMENTS

IN THE PREPARATION of this work I consulted colleagues in other museums and libraries, and for their generous co-operation in all matters relating to the supply of material and information my grateful thanks are due. In particular, I would like to acknowledge the help given by Dr W. G. Archer, O.B.E.; Miss Gira Sarabhai, of the Calico Museum of Textiles, Ahmedabad; Miss Gertrude Townsend, Keeper of Textiles, Museum of Fine Arts, Boston; Mr C. H. Rock, Director of Paisley Museum; Mrs R. Barker, Keeper of Art, Castle Museum, Norwich; Miss Anne Buck, Curator of the Gallery of English Costume, Manchester; Mr C. S. Minto, City Librarian and Curator, Edinburgh; and Mrs A. C. Weibel, of the Detroit Institute of Arts. In problems relating to weaving technique, I consulted the late Mr J. F. Flanagan, formerly of the Royal College of Art.

JOHN IRWIN
May, 1972

FOREWORD

THIS MONOGRAPH is a successor to my earlier one (now out of print) called *Shawls: a study in Indo-European influences*, Her Majesty's Stationery Office, London, 1955. The scope of the first chapter is more or less the same, only minor changes having been made. The second chapter, however, which was formerly entitled 'The Shawl in Europe', has now been narrowed in scope to cover only 'The Kashmir Shawl in Europe: its Influence and Imitation'. This has been considered necessary in view of the subsequent expansion of knowledge about European shawl history, and because more specialized studies by the appropriate authorities are now in preparation.

I have reached this decision in consultation with my colleagues in the Museum's Department of Textiles, and I am especially grateful to Miss N. K. Rothstein and Miss W. E. Hefford for going carefully through the text and making many detailed suggestions. I also have to acknowledge much patient help from Miss B. Tyers of my own Department in preparing the revised material for the printer.

JOHN IRWIN
Keeper, Indian Section
May, 1972

✻ I ✻

THE KASHMIR SHAWL

ORIGIN AND TECHNIQUE

THE ENGLISH WORD 'shawl' is derived from the Persian *shal*, originally denoting a class of woven fabric rather than a particular article of dress. In traditional Indo-Persian usage *shal* could equally well apply to a scarf, a turban, a mantle, or even a coverlet, the distinguishing feature being that the material was fine wool or some other kind of animal fleece. The Italian traveller Pietro della Valle, writing in 1623, observed that whereas in Persia the *scial* or shawl was worn as a girdle, in India it was more usually carried 'across the shoulders'.[1]

Worn by Indians as a shoulder-mantle, the shawl was essentially a male garment; its degree of fineness was traditionally accepted as a mark of nobility. Although a garment so simple in shape and form undoubtedly had a long history not only in India but also in the Near East,[2] the finest brocaded woollen shawls of the modern era are synonymous with the name of Kashmir.

The origins of brocade-weaving in Kashmir are obscure. According to local legend recorded in the first half of the nineteenth century,[3] the founder of the industry was Zain-ul-'Abidin (A.D. 1420–70), whom historians have called the Akbar of Kashmir, in recognition of his enlightened rule and promotion of the arts. Zain-ul-'Abidin was said to have introduced Turkistan weavers for the purpose.[4] This claim has been challenged by the distinguished art historian, Dr Moti Chandra, who believes that brocaded shawls were woven in Kashmir at least as

---

[1] Pietro della Valle, vol. ii, p. 248.

[2] Herodotus, in the fifth century B.C., described Egyptians as wearing a woollen garment in terms which indicate a shawl (Book II, 81).

[3] Baron Charles Hügel, p. 118.

[4] The introduction of new weaving techniques into Kashmir 'from distant countries' during Zain-ul-'Abidin's reign, and that these included woollen fabrics, is confirmed in an early text known as Srivara Pandita's *Rajatarangini*. See Chandra and Agrawala, 'A note on some cultural references in Srivara Pandita's *Rajatarangini*' in *Bulletin of Prince of Wales Museum, Bombay*, no. 7, 1959–62, pp. 35–40.

early as the eleventh century; but, as his evidence hinges upon uncertainties of textual interpretation, it cannot be regarded as conclusive.[5]

The technique of Kashmir shawl-brocading is known to historians as the twill-tapestry weave, because of its basic similarity with the technique traditionally employed in western Europe for tapestry weaving. According to this, the wefts of the patterned part of the fabric were inserted by means of wooden spools (Kashmiri *tojli*), without the use of a shuttle. Weft threads alone form the pattern; these do not run the full width of the cloth, being woven back and forth round the warp threads only where each particular colour is needed. The only significant difference between the technique as employed in Europe and India is that in the former case the ground is a plain weave, whereas in Kashmir it is a twill. On the Indian sub-continent, the nearest parallels are the figured cottons and silks known respectively as *jamdanis*[6] and *chanderis*.[7] However, a distinguishing feature of the manufacture as practised in Kashmir is the independent role of a designer or *naqqāsh*, who was in fact much more highly paid than the weaver. This aspect will be discussed in detail later.

The twill-tapestry technique, as practised by Kashmir shawl-weavers, was slow and laborious and demanded a high degree of specialization. A single shawl with a large area of pattern sometimes took eighteen months or more to complete. However, in the early nineteenth century, when designs became increasingly elaborate, a new practice was introduced of dividing the work of a single shawl among two or more looms. In this way, a design which had formerly occupied one loom for eighteen months could now be produced by two looms in nine months, or by three looms in correspondingly less time. After the various parts of a design had been separately woven, they were handed over to the needle-worker (*rafugar*), who joined them together, the joins being executed with such subtlety and fineness that it is often impossible to detect them with a naked eye. In 1821 William Moorcroft (see pp. 6 & 22) described this method of distributing work among several looms as a recent introduction.[8] He mentioned as many as

---

[5]   M. Chandra, 'Kashmir shawls' in *Bulletin of Prince of Wales Museum, Bombay*, no. 3, 1954, pp. 1–24. Dr Chandra's dating of the shawls reproduced with his article must also be regarded as controversial. In my opinion some are dated much too early.

[6]   P. Jayakar, 'Cotton *jamdanis* of Tanda and Banaras' in *Lalit Kala* (*Journal of Lalit Kala Akademi, New Delhi*), no. 6, 1959, pp. 37–46.

[7]   'Chanderi *saris*' in *Marg*, vol. xv, no. 4, Bombay, 1962, p. 14.

[8]   Moorcroft, MSS. Eur. D.260.

eight looms being engaged on a single shawl; but later in the century this number was often exceeded, and there was one report of a shawl being assembled from 1,500 separate pieces.[9] These are sometimes called 'patchwork shawls'.

Another important innovation introduced at the beginning of the nineteenth century was the *amli* or needleworked shawl, which was ornamented entirely with the needle on a plain woven ground. (It must be added, however, that even the *tilikar* or loom-woven shawls often betray *some* signs of needlework, because a *rafugar* or embroiderer was usually responsible for the final touching-up of the loom-woven pattern. This touching-up sometimes included the reinforcing of colours where needed, and occasionally even more fundamental modifications to the design.) The type of shawl with an *entirely* needleworked pattern, however, was unknown in Kashmir before the nineteenth century. It was introduced at the instigation of an Armenian named Khwāja Yūsuf, who had been sent to Kashmir in 1803 as the agent of a Constantinople trading firm. It had not previously occurred to merchants that simulation of the loom-woven patterns by the much simpler process of needle-embroidery on a plain ground required very much less time and skill, and consequently less outlay. The ingenious Khwāja Yūsuf saw his chance, and with the help of a seamster by the name of 'Ali Bābā produced the first needle-worked imitations for the market at one-third of the cost of the loom-woven shawls.[10] Besides this enormous saving in production costs, the needleworked shawls at first escaped the Government duty levied on the loom-woven shawls, which in 1823 amounted to 26 per cent of the value. As a result, enormous profits were made, and this branch of the industry expanded rapidly. In 1803 there were only a few *rafugars* or embroiderers available with the necessary skill for the work. Twenty years later, there were estimated to be five thousand, many of them having been drawn from the ranks of former landholders,[11] dispossessed of their property by Ranjit Singh in 1819, when Kashmir was invaded and annexed to the Sikh kingdom.

A cloth intended to serve as the ground of an '*amli* or embroidered shawl was first placed on a plank and rubbed with a piece of highly-polished agate or cornelian, until perfectly smooth. After this, the design was transferred from paper to the cloth by pouncing with coloured powder or charcoal. For the

---

9   Colonel J. A. Grant, quoted in *Kashmeer and its shawls* (anonymous), 1875, p. 48.

10   Moorcroft, MSS. Eur. E.113, p. 33.

11   Moorcroft, *op. cit.*

needlework, stem-stitch and satin-stitch were most commonly used; and in order to make the stitches as flat as possible against the ground (and therefore similar to the woven patterns), care was taken to nip up individual threads of the warp in the stitching. Moorcroft described the needlework of the first 'amli shawls as being less perfect and having the raised or embossed appearance of traditional Indian chain-stitch work, the improved method being learned subsequently from embroiderers of Kirman province in Persia.[12] Needleworked shawls were made throughout the nineteenth century, and, apart from those simulating loom-woven patterns, many were made with scenes depicting human figures, which will be discussed later in the section devoted to style. It is important to add here, however, that after about 1850 there was a marked deterioration in the technique of many 'amli shawls—particularly those with human figures—and some of the embroiderers resorted to a comparatively coarse chain-stitch, sometimes executed on a cotton ground.[13]

The material traditionally used for Kashmir shawl-weaving was fleece derived from a Central Asian species of the mountain goat, *Capra hircus*. This was popularly known in the West either as *pashmina* (from Persian *pashm*, meaning in fact any kind of wool) or *cashmere*, from the old spelling of Kashmir. The latter term is particularly misleading, because all shawl-wool used in Kashmir was imported from Tibet or Central Asia in the first place and was not at any time produced locally.[14]

The fleece was grown by the animals as a natural protection against the severities of the winter climate of those regions. It appeared beneath the rough outer hair—the finest being derived from the under-belly—and was shed on the approach of summer. Although goats were the main producers of shawl-wool, a similar fleece was derived from wild Himalayan mountain sheep such as the Shapo (*Ovis orientalis vignei*), the Argali (*Ovis ammon*), the Bharal (*Pseudois nayaur*), and

---

[12]   Moorcroft, MSS. Eur. D.260, p. 4. See also MSS. Eur. E.113 and D.264.

[13]   The fact of the matter is that late 'amli shawls are very variable in quality. A possible explanation is that the coarser kinds were made in the Punjab by less skilled hands.

[14]   To add to the confusion over the use of the term *cashmere*, the British textile trade has now adopted a new definition unrelated to the raw material. According to the Director of the Shirley Institute, Manchester, the term is used 'to describe a certain type of cloth formerly woven from yarns spun from goat fibres', and he includes cloth woven with any high-quality wool yarn. 'The weave must be 2/1 weft twill with a larger number of picks than ends per inch, giving what is also known as the "cashmere twill" or "plain back" weave' (from a letter to the author dated 19.3.1954).

the Himalayan Ibex (*Capra ibex*).[15] It was even claimed that Tibetan shepherds' dogs sometimes grew the same fleece.[16]

Most of the fleece reaching Kashmir belonged to one of two distinct grades. The best and most renowned for its soft silkiness and warmth was known as *asli tūs*, which was derived only from the *wild* animals, collected from rocks and shrubs against which the animals rubbed themselves on the approach of warm weather. The extreme fineness of this grade was probably due to the greater heights at which the animals wintered, and it was this material which gave rise to well-known stories of shawls being so fine that they could be drawn through a thumb-ring—the so-called 'ring-shawls' of Mughal fame.[17] However, the number of shawls woven in pure *asli tūs* was probably never more than a very small proportion of the total, owing to its comparative scarcity, the higher import duties charged upon it, and the much greater time and effort required for its cleaning and spinning. In 1821, the annual imports of *asli tūs* were said to constitute less than one-sixth of the total bulk of other shawl-wool imports, and in the whole of Kashmir there were only two looms specializing exclusively in the weaving of pure *asli tūs*.[18] In the Museum's collection of shawls, there is at least one piece which can almost certainly be said to have been woven with fleece derived from a *wild* animal—probably *Capra hircus laniger*. That is the shawl reproduced at plate 12, known as the 'Thomas Coulson shawl', since it is known to have been acquired by an officer of the English East India Company of that name about the year 1770.[19]

The second grade of shawl-wool was derived from domesticated goats, and this provided the bulk of the yarn for Kashmir looms, at least until the nineteenth century. Prior to 1800, most of it came from Ladakh and Western Tibet. Shortly after the turn of the century, however, there was an epidemic among goats in these areas, and henceforth supplies were derived mainly from herds kept by nomadic Kirghiz tribes and imported through Yarkand and Khotan. In

---

15 Moorcroft, MSS. Eur. E.113.

16 G. T. Vigne, vol. ii, p. 124, and C. E. Bates, p. 55.

17 Manucci, vol. ii, p. 341.

18 Moorcroft, MSS. Eur. D.260, pp. 1–2.

19 Samples were sent for analysis to H. M. Appleyard, Textile Consultant, of Halifax, Yorkshire, who reported as follows: 'The yarns and fibres have been examined microscopically, and the mean fibre has been measured. The yarns are very fine, having from 5 to 8 fibres in a cross-section. The mean fibre diameter is 17·3 μm which is near to that of present-day Iranian cashmere' (quoted from a letter dated 12 May 1972).

the second half of the century the main source was Sinkiang, and in particular Turfan.[20] As supplies at this period were seldom enough to meet demand, goat-fleece became increasingly expensive in relation to other wools. This encouraged adulteration and a general falling off in traditional standards, which was undoubt-edly one of the factors contributing to the decline of the shawl trade in the 1860s, to be discussed later.

ORGANIZATION OF THE INDUSTRY

The earliest detailed account of the Kashmir shawl industry is that written by William Moorcroft between 1820 and 1823, preserved in manuscript at the India Office Library, London. These reveal a situation in which division of labour was far advanced, to the extent of twelve or more independent specialists being involved in the making of a single shawl.

First among these were the spinners, who were women working in their own homes. The raw material was given to them in a very dirty condition, their first task being to separate it into fine fleece, inferior fleece, and hair. The fine fleece constituted only about one-third of the total weight, and this had to be further divided into two grades of fineness, the second being known as *phīri* or seconds wool, which was reserved for inferior shawls. The yarns were spun into lengths of about 2,500 yards, then doubled and twisted, and for this work the spinners earned a maximum of about one and a half annas or three-halfpence a day.[21]

The dyers constituted another separate group, buying and selling yarn inde-pendently. Moorcroft quotes them as saying that in Mughal times more than three hundred tints were in regular use;[22] but by the beginning of the nineteenth century when he was writing, this number had been reduced to sixty-four. Most of these were vegetable dyes: blues and purples from indigo; orange and yellow from carthamus and saffron; reds mainly from logwood. But other sources were also used, including cochineal for crimson, and iron filings for black. Oddly enough, green was said to have been extracted from imported English baizes or broadcloths, which were boiled for the purpose.[23]

Before weaving could begin, at least six other specialists were involved. These

---

[20] B. H. Baden Powell, p. 33f.
[21] Moorcroft, MSS. Eur. E.113, p. 7.
[22] *Ibid.*, Eur. F.38, letter dated 21.5.1820.
[23] Vigne, vol. ii, p. 127; and Moorcroft, MSS. Eur. E.113, p. 10.

were the warp-maker, warp-dresser, warp-threader, pattern-drawer, colour-caller and pattern-master.

It was the warp-maker's job to wind the length of warp to the correct number of threads (usually 2,000 to 3,000 double-threaded warps being required for a shawl); the warp-dresser's to size the warp with starch, and the warp-threader's to pass the yarns through the heddles and reed. The importance of the pattern-drawer, or *naqqāsh* (see illus. no. 2), is indicated by the fact that he received the highest pay—far higher even than that of the weaver.[24] Pattern-drawers were few in number, and in the second half of the century, when the industry was very much expanded, the art was still said to be confined to only five or six families.[25] The pattern-drawer sometimes coloured his own drawing (illus. no. 5), but usually choice and disposition of colour were left to the colour-caller (*tarah gurū*). With a black-and-white drawing before him, the colour-caller, beginning at the bottom and working upwards, called out each colour, the number of warps along which it was required to extend, and so on, until the whole pattern or section of pattern had been covered. This was taken down by the pattern-master (*ta'līm gurū*) and transcribed into a kind of shorthand intelligible to the weaver. An original transcription or *ta'līm* is shown at illus. no. 4, and in the painting reproduced at illus. no. 3 the weavers can be seen working with one before them.

Besides those who prepared the warps of the main part of the shawl, an entirely separate group of specialists prepared the silk warps of the narrow outer borders or edgings. The use of silk warps for these parts was intended to give them more body or stiffness so that the shawl would hang better. However, this had the disadvantage of causing uneven shrinkage and sometimes spoiling the shape of a shawl when washed.

The weavers were all men, foremost among whom were the *ustāds* who owned the looms. The cost of a shawl-loom in the early nineteenth century varied from one and a half to five rupees (approximately 15p to 50p), and a *ustād* might own anything from three to three hundred looms, each normally employing three operators.[26]

There were two main systems of contract between the *ustād* and those who

---

[24] According to Moorcroft, pattern-drawers earned from 2 to 8 annas a day according to skill, compared with the weaver's maximum of 1 anna a day. He calculated 1 anna as being equal to one old penny.

[25] C. E. Bates, p. 56.

[26] Only two operators when a very simple pattern was involved.

worked his looms. One was based on piecework, whereby the weavers received a fixed sum for every hundred spools passed round as many warps (allowing a maximum earning in Moorcroft's time of about one anna or an old penny a day per man, increasing to about double this sum in 1870).[27] A second system was based on partnership, whereby the loom-owner advanced the loom and raw materials and took one-fifth of the net proceeds of sale.

The spools or *tojlis* with which the weavers worked in place of shuttles were made of light, smooth wood and had both ends charred to prevent their becoming rough or jagged in use. Each spool held about three grains of yarn; and the number used in the weaving of a pattern varied from 400 to 1,500, according to degree of elaboration. In the process of weaving, a cloth was faced downwards and the weaver inserted his spools from the reverse side. After each line of weft had been completed to his satisfaction, the comb was brought down 'with a vigour and repetition of stroke which appear disproportionately great to the delicacy of the materials.'[28] One of the ways by which merchants determined the quality or standard of weaving was by counting the number of comb-strokes or wefts to the *girah* (one-sixteenth of a yard).

In 1821 Moorcroft wrote that there were 'sometimes as many as fifty looms in a single house, though more commonly not half this number.'[29] Later in the century, however, a hundred or more looms were sometimes concentrated together. 'I went to inspect one of the largest manufactures in Kashmir,' wrote a traveller in the 1860s. 'The proprietor, a Mohammedan, employs 300 hands. His house is a handsome, three-storied building, well aired and lighted, and the workers are seated at their looms like clerks at their desks . . .'[30]

Moorcroft described the main profit-makers of the industry not as the loom-owners but as the *mohkums* or shawl-brokers, who were intermediaries between the producers and foreign merchants. Later, as the result of the concentration of loom-ownership into fewer hands, there arose a new class in the form of owners of large manufactures, known as *kārkhānādārs*. The term *ustād* was then applied to those who worked as foremen or supervisors for the *kārkhānādār*.[31]

The weavers were the most oppressed section of the industry, the majority

---

[27] C. E. Bates, p. 54.

[28] Moorcroft, MSS. Eur. E.113, p. 17.

[29] *Ibid.*, p. 16.

[30] Colonel Grant, quoted in *Kashmeer and its shawls* (anonymous), p. 48.

[31] C. E. Bates, p. 53.

being depicted as ill-clothed, under-nourished, and permanently in debt. Moorcroft wrote that without the supplementary earnings of wife and children the average weaver could not even support a family.

After Kashmir had been handed over by the British to the Maharaja Gulab Singh in 1846, conditions for the weavers deteriorated even further. The Maharaja levied a poll-tax of Rs. 47–8 per annum on each shawl-weaver;[32] and in order to ensure a constant income from this source he introduced a law forbidding any weaver—whether half-blind or otherwise incapacitated—to relinquish his loom without finding a substitute (a condition almost impossible to fulfil). On top of this, an *ad valorem* duty of 25 per cent was charged on each shawl, and its assessment and collection was farmed out to a corrupt body of officials, whose own illegal exactions were said to have amounted to a further 25 per cent of the value.[33]

In face of such oppression, hundreds of weavers adopted the dangerous course of fleeing the country—an escape made difficult by the limited number of mountain passes and the fact that they were guarded. As a measure of the despair which drove weavers to this course, it must be remembered that it involved deserting their families and the knowledge that they would be victimized as hostages.[34]

Those who successfully escaped settled in Punjab towns such as Lahore, Amritsar, Ludhiana, Nurpur, Gurdaspur, Sialkot, Gujrat, Kangra and Simla, all of which produced their own 'Kashmir' shawls. Shawl-weaving had been established at Lahore (probably by Kashmiri immigrants) at least as early as Akbar's reign (A.D. 1556–1605),[35] and in the mid-seventeenth century the French traveller Bernier also mentioned Agra and Patna in this connection. He added that the shawls woven in these cities were inferior in softness and texture to genuine *kashmirs*, which he attributed to the poorer quality of the water of the plains.[36] A more likely reason was the difficulty of obtaining the best goat-fleece. For centuries Kashmir had monopolized the main sources of supply, and owing to the lack of suitable passes linking Central Asia with the plains of Northern India it was difficult to divert supplies.[37] As a result, shawl-weavers working in the plains were often compelled to adulterate goat-fleece with Kirman sheep's wool.[38]

---

32 A reduction of Rs. 11 was made in 1867.

33 C. E. Bates, pp. 54–7, and R. Thorp, *passim*.

34 R. Thorp, p. 36.

35 *Ain-i-Akbari*, vol. i, p. 32. See also *Pelsaert*, p. 36, and *Manrique*, vol. i, p. 429.

36 Bernier, p. 402.

37 Torrens, p. 93.

38 B. H. Baden Powell, p. 43.

The earliest documentary references to the Kashmir shawl industry appear in literature of Akbar's reign (A.D. 1556–1605), but unfortunately they throw no light on style. In the *Aīn-i-Akbarī*, or Institutes of Akbar, the Emperor is revealed as a keen admirer of the shawls who not only kept his wardrobe well stocked with them but introduced the fashion of wearing them in pairs (*doshāla*), stitched back-to-back, so that the undersides were never visible.[39] From the same source we learn that *kashmirs* were already at this period renowned as gifts and sent to distant countries.[40]

There are indications that the shawls most coveted during the early Mughal period were embellished with gold and silver thread. In 1630, Manrique described the finest examples as having 'borders ornamented with fringes of gold, silver and silk thread. They [the Princes and Nobles] wear them like cloaks, either muffling themselves up in them or else carrying them under their arms. These choice cloths are of white colour when they leave the loom, but are afterwards dyed any hue desired and are ornamented with various coloured flowers and other kinds of decoration, which make them very gay and showy.'[41] Shawls of this type are often mentioned in the early records of the English East India Company as being useful articles of bribery. Sometimes they were offered by native officials to the Europeans, and Sir Thomas Roe, James I's ambassador to the Mughal court, records in characteristic language how he indignantly rejected such a bribe offered by the Governor of Surat soon after his arrival in 1616: 'And pressing me to take a Gold Shalh, I answered we were but newly friends: when I saw any constancy in his carriage and the money paid, I would be more free with him, yet I would receive no obligation . . .'[42]

In 1668, Bernier wrote that shawls measured about 5 ft by $2\frac{1}{2}$ ft and had plain fields, decoration being limited to the end-borders or heads, which were *less than one foot in depth*.[43] This shallowness of the end-borders appears to have been characteristic until the beginning of the nineteenth century, when, as will be shown, they were suddenly enlarged. Thévenot, Bernier's contemporary, men-

---

[39] *Aīn-i-Akbari*, vol. ii, p. 15.

[40] *Ibid.*, vol. i, p. 32.

[41] Manrique, vol. i, pp. 428–9. These, of course, bear no relation to the comparatively coarse shawl-goods embroidered with gold thread 'in Kashmir style', and produced in large quantities in the Punjab in the late nineteenth century.

[42] Roe, p. 223.

[43] Bernier, p. 403.

1. Abdullah Qutb-Shāh of Golconda wearing a Kashmir shawl.
Painted about 1670   *British Museum, Add. MSS. 5254*

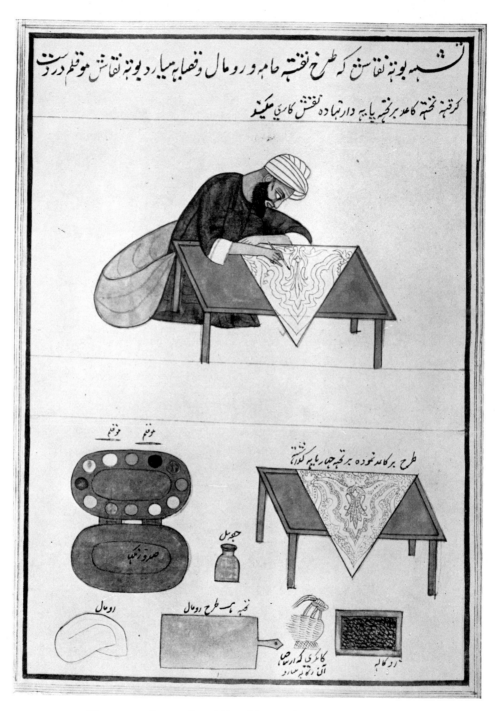

2. The pattern-drawer *(naqqāsh)* and his implements. Painted by a native artist, mid-19th century   *India Office Library, Add. Or. 1704*

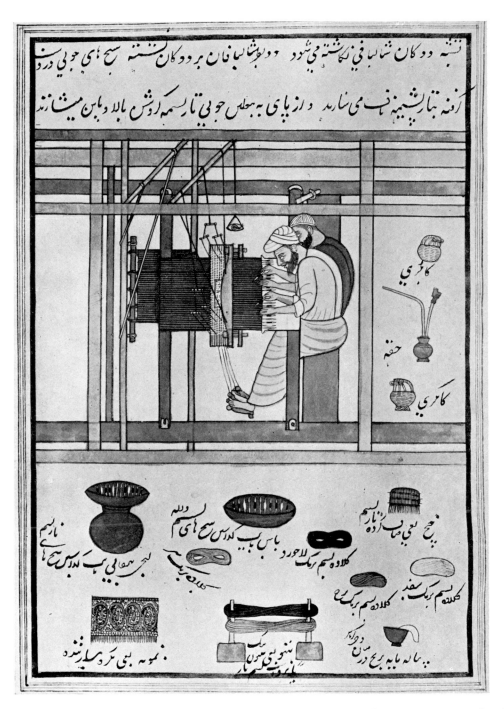

3. Kashmir shawl-loom, with various appliances used in weaving. Painted by a native artist, mid–19th century

India Office Library, Add. Or. 1729

4. *Ta'līm* or coded pattern-guide, as used by Kashmir shawl-weavers. Acquired in Kashmir in 1881
Victoria and Albert Museum, I.M.33–1924

5. Designs from a shawl-weaver's pattern book. Acquired in Kashmir in 1881
Victoria and Albert Museum, I.M.32–1924

tions that the ground colour varied, but that Hindus favoured follimort or dead-leaf (*feuille-morte*).[44]

The earliest surviving shawl-piece in a public collection is a fragment preserved in the Calico Museum of Textiles, Ahmedabad (plate 1 shows a smaller fragment of the same shawl, given by Miss Gira Sarabhai of the Calico Museum to the Victoria and Albert Museum). It consists of part of an end-border with a repeat of delicate, freely-spaced flowering-plants, rendered in the semi-naturalistic style of the late seventeenth century. Shawls with similar end-borders are often depicted in portraits of the Golconda school of painting, a typical example being the portrait of Qutb-Shāh at illus. no. 1, facing p. 10.

FIG. 1. *c*. 1680

FIG. 2. 1700–1730

At this period the characteristic motive of Kashmir shawl-design was a slender flowering plant with roots (fig. 1). It combined the grace and delicacy of Persian floral ornament (from which it was ultimately derived) with the naturalism characteristic of Mughal art. In the early eighteenth century, this simple floral motive was treated more formally, and the number of flowers increased (fig. 2). At about the same time it ceased to be depicted as a flower with roots and merged with another well-known Indo-Persian decorative motive—the conventional vase-of-flowers. Many of the eighteenth century forms betray their dual origin by retaining both the vase and the appearance of root-growth. The name given to these floral motives was *būtā*, meaning literally 'flower', and it was not until the middle of the eighteenth century that the outline of the motive began to harden into the rigid formal shape which later came to be known in the West as

---

44 Thévenot, vol. iii, p. 37.

11

the *cone* or *pine* (but still known in Kashmir as *būṭā*). Although this motive had antecedents in Near Eastern textile patterns of the seventh or eighth centuries A.D.,[45] the cone in the varied forms in which it became associated with shawls was clearly the product of separate development.

Independently of the Kashmir *būṭā*, another type of cone based on the leaf-form appeared more or less simultaneously in Persian decorative art. This Persian form had an important influence on the subsequent development of the Kashmir cone, giving rise to a variety of cone forms which were common to Indo-Persian art of the period.

A further stage was reached in the first quarter of the nineteenth century, when the Kashmir cone began to lose track of its naturalistic, floral origin and became a purely conventional form (fig. 6). This prepared the way for a final stage of abstraction when the cone became elongated and transformed into a scroll-like unit as part of a complicated over-all pattern (fig. 8).

Evidence of the styles of cone fashionable in India, Persia and Turkey in the year 1823 is available in the form of eight signed and dated colour-drawings acquired by the Metropolitan Museum of Art, New York, in 1962.[46] These are

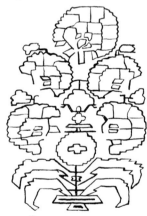

FIG. 3. 1720–1750

FIG. 4. 1740–1770

included among the thirty-four drawings which Moorcroft despatched from Kashmir to England in that year and are reproduced at illus. nos. 6–13.

As guides to dating, the different stages in the development of the cone must be regarded with caution. Because a certain form came into vogue at a certain period,

---

[45] O. Falke, fig. 35; and A. C. Weibel, fig. 51.

[46] C. Karpinski, 'Kashmir to Paisley' in *Bulletin of the Metropolitan Museum of Art*, New York, November, 1963, pp. 116–24. Two of the drawings are reproduced in colour.

it did not necessarily follow that earlier types were superseded. In fact, it often happened that the older well-tried motives and patterns outlived the new.

Kashmir shawls were first worn in fashionable circles in the West in the third quarter of the eighteenth century, and by 1800 the shawl trade between Kashmir and the West was well established. The appearance of European agents in Kashmir added fresh colour to an already cosmopolitan scene. 'At this city,' wrote Moorcroft from the capital, Srinagar, in 1822, 'I find merchants from Gela and from other cities of Chinese Turkestan, from Uzbeck, Tartary, from Kabul, from Persia, from Turkey, and from the provinces of British India engaged in purchasing and in waiting for the getting up of shawl goods differing as to quality and pattern *in conformity to the taste of the markets for which they are intended* in a degree probably not suspected in Europe.'[47] Some indication of the diversity of tastes for which the Kashmiri weaver catered is indicated by the descriptions of shawl-goods given in Appendix 2, compiled by Moorcroft during his three-year investigation into the shawl industry. In the preparation of designs for the Western market, one merchant in particular—an Armenian named Khwāja

FIG. 5. 1770–1800

FIG. 6. 1815 onwards

Yūsuf (already mentioned as the originator of the *'amli* or needleworked shawl, p. 3)—appears to have had an important influence. He had been sent to Kashmir in 1803 by a trading firm at Constantinople, in order to have shawls made according to patterns that he took with him.[48]

---

47 Moorcroft, MSS. Eur. G.28, letter dated 12 November 1822.

48 Tessier, p. 27.

Khwāja Yūsuf's original idea in introducing the needleworked shawl was to simulate and undersell the loom-woven patterns. About 1830, however, the needleworkers began producing a distinct style of design with human figures, usually illustrating one of the well-known poetical romances of Indo-Persian literature, such as the *Khamsa* ('Five Poems') of Nizami (*see* pl. 27), and the *'Iyār-i-dānish* ('Criterion of Knowledge') of Abu'l Fazl. It was said that Ranjit Singh (who held dominion over Kashmir from 1819 to 1839) especially admired this type of shawl and advanced five thousand rupees for a pair to be worked with scenes illustrating his victories (only one of which was completed).[49] In the second half of the century *'amli* shawls were sometimes embroidered in the form of a pictorial map of the capital, Srinagar, a fine example being included in the Museum's collection (pls. 42–4).[50]

FIG. 7. 1820–1830

FIG. 8. 1850–1870

The nineteenth-century popularity of the Kashmir shawl in Europe undoubtedly owed much to romantic associations with the 'mysterious and unchanging East'. The new popular journalism of the period was always ready to foster such associations, and this led to the publication of innumerable articles by unqualified authorities setting out to explain the alleged antiquity of Kashmir motives and patterns and even ascribing to them an elaborate symbolism. Typical of them is an article which appeared in the magazine *Household Words*, founded by Charles Dickens: 'If an article of dress could be immutable, it would be the

[49]   Vigne, p. 124.
[50]   Another map-shawl, embroidered in 1870, was published in the *Magazine of Art*, vol. 25, London, 1901, pp. 452–53.

[Kashmir] shawl; designed for eternity in the unchanging East; copied from patterns which are the heirlooms of caste; and woven by fatalists, to be worn by adorers of the ancient garment, who resent the idea of the smallest change . . .'[51] Repetition of such nonsense over a long period had its effect. On the one hand, it belied the true character of the Kashmir industry as a living and developing tradition adaptable to changing conditions; and on the other, it obscured the important influence exercised upon those changes by European taste.

One way of tracing the development of Kashmir designs in the nineteenth century is by examining shawls depicted in contemporary European portrait painting and costume engravings. These show that the shawl most popular in the first two decades was of rectangular shape with a plain field and large semi-naturalistic floral cones in the borders.[52] Examples are often depicted in French portraits of the period, particularly in the works of Ingres. Shawls feature in his portraits of Mme Rivière (1805), Mme la Comtesse de Tournon (1812), Mme de Senonnes (1814), Baronne Popenheim (1818), and the Stamaty Family (1818).[53]

A distinctive feature of the cone at this period was its streamer-like bending tip, reminiscent of the earlier cypress-and-almond-tree motive of Persian art.[54] By 1815 the semi-naturalistic floral cone had begun to give way to a more formal, abstract type (figs. 6 and 7). Shawls with a diapered or trellised field were also coming into favour, and among these was the square shawl with a medallion in the centre and quarter medallions at each corner, known as the chand-dār or 'moon shawl' (pls. 15, 18, 19). In 1823, Moorcroft remarked that Persian taste favoured shawls in which the pattern 'almost completely covers and conceals the colour of the ground'; and this probably refers to shawls of the type shown at plates 24 and 25.

The mid-nineteenth century was a period of great prosperity for the merchants and dealers, and also one of artistic decline, when foreign taste increasingly dominated shawl design. The French were the main instigators, and it was in the year 1850 that the first French agents arrived in Kashmir with a mission to 'improve' the traditional designs.[55] In the following decade many visitors to

---

[51]   *Household Words*, 28 August 1852.

[52]   The French shawl merchant Rey, writing in 1823, stated that prior to this period the cone was never more than nine inches in height (J. Rey, p. 146).

[53]   Most of these are reproduced by R. Rosemblum, *Ingres*, London, 1967.

[54]   Textile historians usually refer to this motive as the cypress 'bent by the wind'; but in fact it represents the natural form of the tree, the topmost shoot of which always bends.

[55]   B. H. Baden Powell, p. 41.

Kashmir reported—sometimes with approval but more often with alarm—that 'French patterns and new colours, such as magenta, are beginning to prevail over the genuine Indian designs.'[56] One of these accounts is perhaps worth quoting in full:

'The great estimation in which Cashmere shawls are held in France, and the consequent demand for them, have induced some of the large houses in that country to keep agents in Srinugger [Srinagar, capital of Kashmir]. One result of this is that the French design patterns in Paris and send them out to Cashmere for execution. Although these designs are all in the oriental style, they are no improvement upon the old work of the natives . . . "The French patterns," says Mr Simpson, who brought to the country an experienced artistic eye, "were perhaps purer than the old; they contained more free and sweeping lines, but they wanted the mediaeval richness of the native taste. It may be described as the difference between a piece of Rococo ornament and what an artist of the thirteenth century would have produced. There was a distinguishing character about the original style which is being rubbed out by this foreign influence".'[57]

From other accounts we learn that the weavers themselves resented this foreign interference. 'At first (and in fact until within a few years) much difficulty was experienced in persuading the native designers to alter or amend their patterns. They were attached to their old style and would not accept alteration; but now this difficulty has been overcome and the weavers are willing to adopt hints, in fact they now seldom begin to work till the pattern has been inspected or approved by the agent for whom they work.'[58]

Although Simpson's explanation of the French contribution to Kashmir design is not very clear in expression or terminology, it nevertheless gives important clues. In referring to the 'mediaeval richness' of the traditional as opposed to the French patterns he probably had in mind the marginal ornament of mediaeval European illuminated manuscripts, before which the eye is made to wander restlessly, in convolutions, in marked contrast to what he calls the 'free and sweeping lines' of the French or 'rococo' style, so characteristic of the late designs of both Kashmir and European shawls.

---

[56] Colonel J. A. Grant, quoted in *Kashmeer and its shawls* (anonymous), p. 48.

[57] W. Simpson, *India ancient and modern*, p. 5. Simpson, a well-known English water-colourist, visited Kashmir in 1860 to paint shawl weavers and embroiderers. Two of his paintings are reproduced in the above work.

[58] Letter from Amritsar shawl agent, quoted by B. H. Baden Powell, p. 41.

European intervention in the preparation of designs was so general at this period that when Kashmir shawls were shown at the contemporary international exhibitions of 'art and manufactures', the European agent who commissioned a shawl was given full credit for the design. At the Exhibition of Punjab manufactures held at Lahore in 1873, first prize was awarded to an Amritsar shawl designed by an Englishman, Mr R. Chapman.[59]

Sometimes, when a merchant was dissatisfied with a finished shawl, he cut out certain sections of the pattern and ordered others to be substituted. In this way, the whole appearance of a shawl was sometimes changed while in the merchant's hands.[60]

In the 1860s Kashmir produced the reversible shawl, the pattern being identical on both sides of the cloth. This did not reflect any significant departure in technique, but was achieved by skilful trimming of the loose weft threads on the reverse side, and the outlining of all the main details in the pattern by needlework. The example at plate 37 was shown at the Paris Exhibition of 1867 and bears its original exhibition label which reads: 'Scarf of quite a new fabric. Shows the same on both sides. Sent by Diwan Kirpa Ram,[61] Kashmir. Price: £37 12s 0d.'

From about the second quarter of the nineteenth century Kashmir had to face competition from Persia;[62] but lacking the former's longer experience of patterned shawl-weaving, the Persians were never able to produce shawls of comparable quality. There were two types of Persian shawl which have to be mentioned. The first is woven in the same twill-tapestry technique, the patterns being influenced by those of Kashmir but at the same time distinguished by bolder floral treatment and a more architectural emphasis in design. Moreover, the predominant colour is a rather deep red not at all characteristic of Kashmir. A few specimens of this type survive in museum collections, usually in the form of coverlets or prayer-mats.[63]

---

[59] B. H. Baden Powell, p. 45. The particular shawl is reproduced in the forementioned work, facing p. 45.

[60] B. H. Baden Powell, p. 46.

[61] This was the name of the Prime Minister of Kashmir at that time.

[62] Describing Kirman province, the French traveller Dubeux remarked '. . . on y voit un grand nombre de manufactures de chales qui imitent ceux du Caschmir' (*La Perse*, p. 57).

[63] Examples in the Victoria and Albert Museum (Textile Dept.) are T.41–1932, T.39–1912, 1061–75, 1061a–75, and 346–1880.

The second type of Persian shawl which competed with Kashmir in the nineteenth century was known as the *Hussain Qūli Khān*. These are even more easily distinguishable by the fact that they were woven in silk on harness-looms, the unused sections of the wefts on the underside being left floating.

THE FINAL COLLAPSE

Between 1850 and 1860, shawl exports to Europe more than doubled, far exceeding the total estimated output of the whole industry at the beginning of the century.[64] In the following decade, however, there was a sudden contraction in the market. The average Kashmir shawl of that time (such as the example shown at plate 40) was no longer equal to the best products of the Jacquard looms of Lyons and Paisley and yet was more expensive to buy. On top of this decline came the Franco-Prussian War of 1870–71, resulting in the closure of the French market for *kashmirs*, and the simultaneous and quite sudden eclipse of the shawl as an article of fashion. From being the pride of every girl at her marriage and coming-of-age, the shawl was relegated to the grandmother's wardrobe. As a result, the Kashmir industry, so long geared to Western demands, was doomed. Collapse of trade was followed by the severe famine of 1877–9, when shawl-weavers are said to have 'died like flies'. Most of the survivors, having hands so refined and delicately adjusted to the technique of shawl-weaving that they were useless for most other occupations, subsequently died in destitution.[65] Only the needle-workers experienced temporary respite, adapting themselves to the embroidering of coverlets, table-cloths and similar goods for the tourist market. Within a generation of its final phase of prosperity the shawl industry was dead, and the art of its weavers irrecoverably lost.

---

[64] The export figures were £171,000 in 1850–51, and £351,000 in 1860. Estimates of the earlier output are based on Moorcroft MSS. Eur. E.113, p. 29.

[65] According to evidence handed down verbally, some Kashmir shawl weavers were recruited for carpet-knotting.

🎇 2 🎇

THE KASHMIR SHAWL IN EUROPE:
ITS INFLUENCE AND IMITATION

SHOULDER-MANTLES became fashionable wear in western Europe in the second half of the eighteenth century; but they were at first mostly home-woven in light materials, often plain muslin. The introduction of decorative woollen shawls from Kashmir coincided with the early development of this fashion, but there is no evidence that they initiated it.

Perhaps the earliest reference to the Indian woollen shawl being worn in Europe is in one of Laurence Sterne's letters to Eliza, dated 1767.[1] Eliza, of course, had then recently arrived in London from India, and it would be in keeping with her character to suppose that she herself might have initiated the Western fashion by bringing with her a selection of *kashmirs* when she sailed from Bombay in 1765. However that may be, we know that shortly after this the fashion caught on.[2] Its main attraction at this stage was its warmth and unrivalled softness of texture—qualities which British woollen manufacturers noted with envy, and were soon inspired to try to equal.

There is evidence to suggest that Britain may have been ahead of France in attempting to produce a woollen shawl to compete with the *kashmir*. The pioneering centre was Norwich, where experiments were made in the 1780s in blending Spanish and Norfolk flockwools.[3] At this stage the patterns were needleworked, a good example surviving in the form of a valance at Blickling Hall, Norfolk (now owned by the National Trust). Another, described as a 'Shawl counterpane . . . equal in beauty and far superior in strength to the India counterpanes', was awarded a prize by the Royal Society of Arts in 1791.[4] Edinburgh weavers were perhaps the first to imitate Kashmir shawls in pattern as well as texture, and this they achieved by a brocading technique. Unfortunately

---

[1] Letter 193, dated 30 March 1767, in *Letters of Laurence Sterne*, ed. L. P. Curtis, Oxford, at the Clarendon Press, 1935.

[2] *Philosophical Transactions* (Royal Society), vol. 67, pt 2, 1778, letter dated 17 April 1777.

[3] *Transactions* (Society of Arts), vol. vii, 1789, pp. 167 ff.

[4] *Ibid.*, vol. x, 1792, pp. 196 ff.

none of the brocaded Edinburgh imitations are known to have survived, and it is doubtful whether the cost of production would have made commercial success possible. About 1803 both Norwich and Edinburgh weavers began imitating *kashmirs* in the harness loom, employing silk warps and woollen wefts. By 1808 Paisley weavers were competing in the same way; and in 1812 they made an important advance with the introduction of the 'ten-box lay'[5]—a device which allowed five shuttles to be held in the loom simultaneously, thus greatly facilitating the weaving of multi-coloured patterns in the harness-loom. As a result, Paisley weavers were able to make close copies of Kashmir patterns. Agents were then posted to London to trace the latest shawl designs as they arrived from India. These tracings were despatched at once to Paisley; and within another eight days imitations were being sold in London. The Paisleys were priced at about £12, in competition with the originals at £70 or £100. So successful was this enterprise that by 1818 Paisley imitations were reaching markets as far afield as Turkey and Persia.[6] Paisley manufacturers even tried exporting to India. In the following year several consignments were despatched with this end in view, and in Moorcroft's letters written from India in 1820 and 1821 there are accounts of how they were received: 'At first sight the Shawl Merchants of this country were deceived, but on handling them a look of surprise has spread over their countenances, and on closer examination they discovered that the shawls were not of Kashmeeree fabric. They gave great credit to British artists for their close imitations, but considered them as inferior to the Kashmeeree originals, and exhibited substantial reasons in support of their opinion. They showed with obvious gratification the superior softness, fullness and richness of feel of Kashmeeree over British shawl-cloth, of equal number of thicknesses of thread. This superiority, which must be admitted by a candid examiner, arises from the greater softness of the goat wool and from a looser twist in the Kashmeeree yarn . . .'[7]

Not to be outdone, the next hope of British manufacturers was to obtain independent supplies of the precious goat-fleece believed to give Kashmir weavers their special advantage.

Direct trade with Tibet or Central Asia was not at that time a practical proposition. For centuries the very limited supplies of shawl-wool coming from that

---

[5] *New statistical account of Scotland*, 1845, p. 271; and *Paisley Herald*, 12 November 1859. Both sources state that the 'ten-box lay' was introduced from Manchester.

[6] *The Weavers' Magazine*, 20 October 1818.

[7] MSS. Eur. F.38, letter dated 21 May 1820. Moorcroft implied that Norwich as well as Paisley shawls were reaching India.

source had been monopolized by Kashmiri merchants, and in recent times this monopoly had been confirmed by treaty between Kashmir and Ladakh—the small principality bordering Western Tibet (now part of Kashmir) through which most of the supplies passed. Under pressure from British shawl manufacturers, the East India Company in 1819 commissioned George Rutherford, an officer in their service, to investigate possibilities of diverting supplies into British India; but these efforts met with little success. The few bales he managed to secure were shipped to England between 1821 and 1823, only for the manufacturers to discover that the precious fleece had become so thickly felted with coarse hairs in transit that it could not be economically separated.[8] The financial loss incurred as a result discouraged the Company from making further efforts in this direction.

Supplies from Tibet and Central Asia being impracticable, the alternative was to try naturalizing the shawl-goat in Britain. This had been thought of as early as 1774, when Warren Hastings (himself a keen admirer of Kashmir shawls, many of which he bought for his wife)[9] commissioned George Bogle to visit Tibet and to procure 'one or more pairs of the animal called *tūs*, which produce the shawl wool'.[10] At this stage neither Hastings nor Bogle was aware that the animal they named after its wool (*tūs*) was in fact a goat. Nor apparently was the Teshu Lama of Tibet, for in response to Bogle's request he supplied only sheep.[11] In 1783, Hastings sent another mission to Tibet; this time knowing what nature of animal was concerned. Captain Samuel Turner, who led the expedition, procured a number of goats; but when brought down into the hot plains of Bengal the animals were at once afflicted with a 'cutaneous eruptive humour' from which most of them died. The few survivors were shipped to England but arrived so sickly that they all 'very shortly after perished'.[12] Eight years later the idea of importing the goats was again revived, this time by the newly-founded Society for the Improvement of British Wool. Sir John Sinclair, its energetic president, wrote to everyone in a position of influence whom he thought might help, including such unlikely individuals as Sir William Jones, the eminent

8   *Transactions* (Society of Arts), vol. 46, 1828, p. 131.

9   S. C. Grier, *passim*. A pair of gloves woven in Kashmiri shawl-cloth and formerly belonging to Hastings is preserved at the Indian Institute, Oxford.

10   G. Bogle, p. 8.

11   *Philosophical Transactions* (Royal Society), vol. 67, pt 2, 1778, letter dated 17 April 1777.

12   Samuel Turner, pp. 356–57.

Sanskrit scholar.[13] However, Sinclair's perseverance eventually brought results. In 1793, the Directors of the East India Company notified him that their agents at Bussora, in Persia, had procured 'two animals that produce the shawl-wool.'[14] They arrived in England the same year and were sent first to the private zoo at Earl's Court, London, owned by John Hunter, the famous surgeon.[15] It was intended that Hunter should make some crossing experiments before forwarding them to Sinclair in Scotland, but this plan was frustrated by the early death of the female without progeny. Nothing more is heard of the male, except that it was exhibited to the delight of the crowds at the carnival of St Bartholomew at Smithfield, under the description of 'a savage beast . . . snared on the lofty and barbarous mountains of Thibet.'[16]

It is a coincidence that about this time William Moorcroft, who has been extensively quoted in the first chapter in connection with his investigations into the Kashmir shawl industry between 1820 and 1823, arrived in London from the north of England, a young man of twenty-four, to seek Hunter's advice about his career. Since he had already received some medical training at an infirmary, Hunter advised him to specialize as a veterinary surgeon.[17] Moorcroft followed Hunter's advice, and it was in this capacity that he was sent to India by the East India Company. Whether or not he had actually seen the shawl-goats in Hunter's zoo, there is no doubt that from an early stage he had nursed the ambition of successfully naturalizing them in Britain. Encouragement, both official and non-official, was never lacking. In 1808 (the year Moorcroft left for India) there appeared in a publication of the Board of Agriculture the colourful statement that successful naturalization of the shawl-goat 'would offer a richer prize to our manufacturers than the acquisition of the golden fleece.'[18]

In 1812, Moorcroft got permission to lead an expedition into Western Tibet and returned with fifty shawl-goats.[19] On being embarked for England, however,

[13] Jones replied that he was much too busy to help, being 'engaged from morning to night in arranging the new digest of Indian laws' (*Life, writings and correspondence*, p. 208).

[14] These were almost certainly local Kirman goats, not the authentic shawl-goat. Kirman goats had provided fleece for the 'shawles' sent to England in the seventeenth century (see p. 10); and in the 1670s unsuccessful attempts had been made to establish a colony of these goats on the island of St Helena (*India Office Archives*, Letter Book V, *passim*).

[15] T. Baird, p. 25.

[16] J. Foot, p. 10.

[17] H. H. Wilson, p. xx.

[18] R. Bakewell, pp. 108–09

[19] *Asiatic Researches* (Asiatic Society of Bengal), vol. xii, 1816.

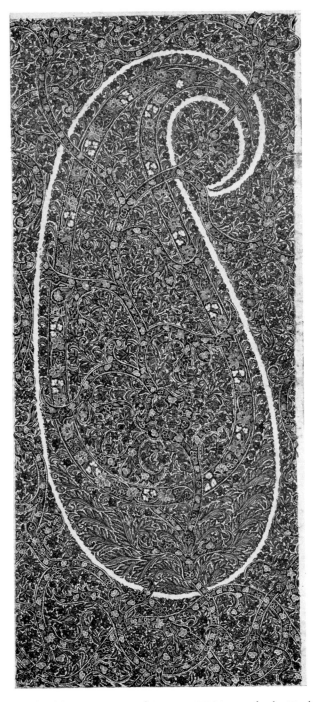

6. Design brought to England by W. Moorcroft in 1823. Writing on back: *Zurdee Kaphooree. By order of Mahummud Azeen Khan, Russia*. With the 7 drawings which follow, this is in the Metropolitan Museum of Art, New York, Elisha Whittelsey Fund, 1962

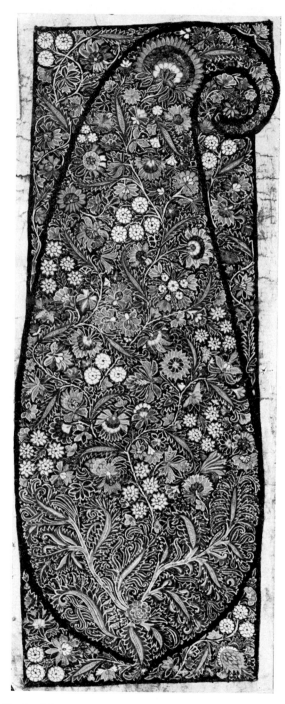

7. Design brought to England by W. Moorcroft in 1823. Writing on back: *Mooshkee. By order of Shooguoob Moolkh, Persia. For Duslar*

8. Design brought to England by W. Moorcroft in 1823. Writing on back: *Logwardee. By order of Shah Zuman, Persia*

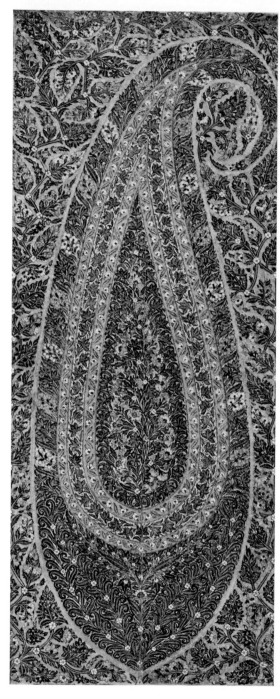

9. Design brought to England by W. Moorcroft in 1823. Writing on back: *Khakee. By order of Shah Zuman, Persia*

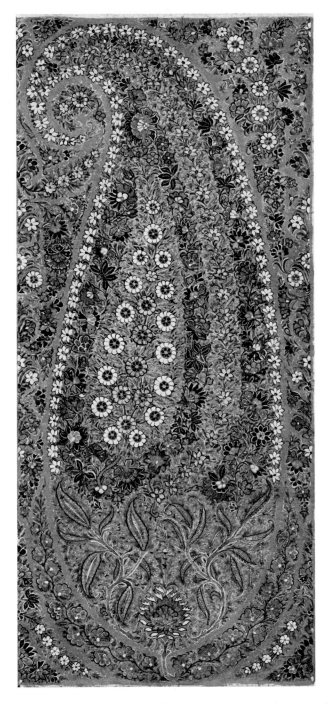

10. Design brought to England by W. Moorcroft in 1823. Writing on back: *Gooleanor. Hindoostan*

11. Design brought to England by W. Moorcroft in 1823. Writing on back: *Pheerozee. By order of Mahummed Azeem Khan, Russia*

12. Design brought to England by W. Moorcroft in 1823. Writing on back: *Colour Zunga. By order of Mahummed Azeen Khan, Russia*

13. Design brought to England by W. Moorcroft in 1823. Writing on back: *Tilace. Hindoostan*

the male animals were segregated on one ship and the females on another. This proved a blunder, for the ship carrying the females was wrecked with total loss on the way home. Of the lonely male goats which arrived in the other ship, the majority were sick and dying, and only four survived the last stage of the journey to Blair, in Scotland, where they were to be kept on the estate of the Duke of Atholl. Within a few months even these died, and once again the experiment ended in total failure.[20]

The next and most ambitious attempt of all was made under French auspices. M. Guillaume Louis Ternaux, a well-known shawl manufacturer, obtained the semi-official support of the French Government to sponsor an expedition to Tibet to acquire a flock of goats. The expedition was led by M. Amédée Joubert, a Turkish language professor at the Bibliothèque Royale, who was already well known as a traveller.[21] Joubert left France in 1818 and travelled first to Turkey, then Russia. On reaching Astrakhan, he was told that there was no need to go to Tibet, because goats of similar species were kept by Kirghiz tribes on the steppes of Western Kazakhstan. Satisfied with the evidence produced for him, he bought 1,289 animals and turned for home. By the time he reached France most of the goats had died; the rest suffered severely from a scab disease similar to that which had afflicted shawl-goats in Britain. However, between two and three hundred recovered sufficiently to be made the subject of experiments. Of these, two pairs were bought by an Englishman, Mr Tower, for separate trials in Essex.[22] Initial results on both sides of the Channel were disappointing. The yield of fleece was extremely low, the male goats averaging about 4 ozs. per year, and the females only half this amount. At this rate, there was little prospect of home supply ever becoming an economic proposition, although, on the grounds of quality alone, there was some satisfaction. In 1828, when Mr Tower's original flock had increased to twenty-seven, sufficient fleece was obtained for three shawls. These were subsequently woven by Messrs Millar & Sons, of Paisley, and were widely admired, one of them being awarded a Gold Medal by the Society of Arts.[23]

Meanwhile experiments were being made in France by crossing the Russian species with Angora goats. This increased by five times the quantity of fleece

20 *Brande's Journal*, vol. 9, p. 330; *Quarterly Review*, July 1820; and *Calcutta Government Gazette*, 10 May 1821.
21 Tessier, p. 25.
22 *Transactions* (Society of Arts), vol. 46, 1828, p. 130.
23 *Transactions* (Society of Arts), vol. 46, 1828, p. 131.

produced,[24] and although unable to fulfil more than a very small fraction of the demands of French industry, these goats continued to be a source of shawl-wool for some years.

Joubert's expedition was the last serious attempt to naturalize the shawl-goat in Europe. But the idea was never entirely dropped, and in 1846, when the British Government made over Kashmir as an independent state to the Maharaja Gulab Singh and his heirs, the transfer was conditional upon an annual tribute of 'one horse, twelve perfect shawl-goats of approved breed (six males and six females), and three pairs of Cashmere shawls.'[25] The tribute of goats was later commuted for a small money payment; but the tribute of shawls continued throughout Queen Victoria's reign (it was said that she bestowed them upon her ladies-in-waiting) and was rescinded on the accession of Edward VII.

To the indefatigable Moorcroft, obsessed with the idea of making British shawls supreme over all competitors, it was not enough to be defeated in attempts to naturalize the shawl-goat. With the same zeal he embarked upon a campaign to naturalize (or at least to promote the immigration of) whole families of Kashmiri spinners, weavers and pattern-drawers. The campaign never bore fruit, but, as the story includes much of interest to the student of the period, excerpts from his correspondence have been included in Appendix 2.

Although British manufacturers pioneered the imitation of Kashmir shawls in Europe, they were eventually overtaken by the French who, in the second quarter of the nineteenth century, were first to exploit for shawl-weaving the revolutionary invention of the Jacquard loom. With the introduction of the Jacquard machine, operations which had previously depended upon one or more drawboys working with the weaver at the harness-loom were now automatically directed by perforated cards, on the same principle as the barrel-organ or pianola. The actual harness of the loom worked as before, but the weaver's task was greatly simplified, particularly in the weaving of elaborate patterns. This innovation profoundly influenced the design of shawls and encouraged the development of much more complicated patterns covering larger areas of the surface of the shawl—a development which in turn influenced the design of shawls in Kashmir.

Jacquard-woven designs characteristic of the 1840s were distinguished by elongated, multiple cones running from edge to centre and leaving only about

---

[24] *Ibid.*, vol. 49, 1833, p. 49.
[25] Article X of the Treaty of 16 March 1846.

half the centre-field plain. These were succeeded in the 1850s by cone-shawls, in what was known as the French 'all-over' pattern. In this the whole ground is figured with the exception of a small area in the centre. These shawls sometimes exceeded twelve feet in length, and individual repeat units of the design sometimes covered as much as a quarter of the whole ground. Their intricacy of detail marked the final triumph of the Jacquard machine.

In the 1850s and 1860s an extremely complex situation was reached in the international shawl trade. On the one hand, the Kashmir industry was largely under the domination of French merchants who had settled there, bringing with them their own pattern-books for native designers to copy. At the same time, France was producing so-called *kashmirs* which were often a decade ahead of the Indian-made designs they were supposed to be imitating, and these in turn were being copied or adapted at other European centres such as Paisley. In spite of this, the idea of a genuine *kashmir* as opposed to a European imitation still retained its associations of superiority, and this explains why some Jacquard weavers in the West went as far as to simulate Persian lettering on their shawls, to give them an added note of authenticity.

The last refinement introduced in Europe was the *reversible* shawl which probably came as an answer to the reversible shawls of Kashmir, first made about 1865 (pl. 37). The European reversibles were made on the Jacquard loom with a double set of warps, the repeat sections of the pattern being ingeniously composed so that opposite sides of the cloth were complementary to one another. The redundant weft threads, when not engaged in the pattern on either face of the cloth, were left floating between the two surfaces.

As explained in the first chapter, the Franco-Prussian War (1870–71) marked the eclipse of the shawl as an article of fashion in the West. More accurately, it should be said that it marked its eclipse as a *luxury* fashion only, for one of the factors which contributed to its abandonment in upper-class circles was undoubtedly its increasing popularity among the lower classes. By 1870 a Jacquard-woven Paisley shawl could be bought for as little as £1,[26] and the identical pattern printed on cotton for only a few shillings. Thus, the Kashmir style, originally a mark of exclusiveness and exotic rarity, had now become vulgar and mundane as a result of its popularity. The surprising thing is that this process took as long as a hundred years.

26 In 1860, the *average* price of a large Paisley harness shawl was 27s, and the cheapest were 17s 6d (Paisley Museum and Art Gallery, *Letters and other papers relating to the evidence given to the Conseil Supérieur . . .* : see Bibliography under MSS.).

APPENDIX I

An account of Shawl-Goods produced in Kashmir in 1823
Compiled from Moorcroft MSS. Eur. E.113 and D.264[1]

TRADE NAME	REMARKS	MANUFAC-TURER'S PRICE	MARKETS
Do-Shāla (or shawls in pairs) *Pattū pashmīna*	Sometimes made of *asli tūs*, but more often of the coarser kinds of shawl wool. Length 4 *gaz*, breadth 1⅞ *gaz*.[2] This is thick and is used as a blanket or for outer clothing	From 5 to 6 rupees per *gaz*	Kashmir, Afghanistan
Shāla phīri	As its name denotes, it is made of *phīri* or seconds wool. Length from 3½ to 4 *gaz*, breadth 1½ *gaz*	From 20 to 30 rupees per piece	Kashmir
Hulwān	Plain white cloth of fine shawl-wool without flower border or other ornament, differs in length but is 12 *girahs* in[3] breadth and is used for turbans and for dyeing	From 3 to 6 rupees per *gaz*	Kashmir, Hindustan, Persia, Afghanistan, etc.
Jauhar shala sada	A shawl with a narrow edging of coloured yarn. From 3½ to 3¾ *gaz* in length, and 1½ in breadth	From 50 to 60 rupees per piece[4]	Kashmir, Hindustan, etc.
Shāla hāshiyadār	Edged by a single border. 3½ *gaz* in length, and 1½ *gaz* in breadth	From 60 to 70 rupees per piece	Kashmir, Hindustan, etc.

---

[1] I am indebted to Mr R. W. Skelton, Deputy Keeper, Indian Section, Victoria and Albert Museum, for help in the revision of transliterations.

[2] The standard, or *ilāhi*, *gaz* was 33 inches.

[3] A *girah* was one-sixteenth of a yard.

[4] MSS. Eur. D.264 reads 'per pair'.

TRADE NAME	REMARKS	MANUFAC-TURER'S PRICE	MARKETS
Shāla do-hāshiyadār	With a double border. Same measurements	From 40 or 60 to 70 rupees per piece	Kashmir, Hindustan, etc.
Shāla chahār hāshiyadār	With four borders. Same measurements	From 60 to 70 rupees per piece	Kashmir, Hindustan, etc.
Hāshiyadār khosar or Khalīl khānī	With two borders and two tunga, sometimes with, at others without, a flower in the corners. Same measurements	From 40 to 50 rupees per piece	Afghanistan
Hāshiyadār kunguradār	This has a border of unusual form with another within side, or nearer to the middle, resembling the crest of the Wall of Asiatic forts furnished with narrow niches or embrasures for Wall pieces, or Matchlocks, whence its name. Same measurements	From 100 to 150 rupees a pair	Hindustan, etc.
Daurdār	With an ornament running all round the shawl between the border and the field. Same measurements	From 100 to 2,300 rupees a pair	Hindustan, Russia
Matandār	With flowers or decorations in the middle of the field. Same measurements	From 300 to 1,800 rupees a pair	Hindustan, Turkey
Chand-dār	With a circular ornament or moon in the centre of the field. Same measurements	From 500 to 2,500 rupees a pair	Hindustan, Turkey, etc.
Chauthidār	With four half-moons. Same measurements	From 300 to 1,500 rupees a pair	Hindustan
Kunjbūtedār	With a group of flowers at each corner. Same measurements	From 200 to 900 rupees a pair	Hindustan, Afghanistan, Persia
Alifdār	With green sprigs without any other colour on a white ground. Same measurements	From 120 to 150 rupees a pair	Hindustan, but more especially Peerzadas [sic]

TRADE NAME	REMARKS	MANUFAC-TURER'S PRICE	MARKETS
Kuddhar	With large groups of flowers somewhat in the form of the cone of a pine with the ends or points straight or curved downwards. Same measurements	—	—
Do-kuddhar	With two rows of such groups. Same measurements	From 100 to 800 rupees a pair	Hindustan
Se-kuddhar	With three rows of the same	From 100 to 800 rupees a pair	Hindustan
Chahar-kuddhar	With four rows of the same[5]	From 200 to 600 rupees a pair	Hindustan
Jāmawārs (or gown-pieces)	Sold in lengths of $3\frac{3}{4}$ *gaz* by $1\frac{1}{2}$ *gaz*		
Khukhabutha (*Kokā-būtā*?)	Large compound flowers, consisting of groups of smaller ones	From 300 to 1,500 rupees per piece	Used by the Persians and Afghans
Rezabūtā	Small flowers thickly set	From 200 to 700 rupees per piece	Kashmir, Hindustan, Afghanistan
Jāl-dār	Net-work	From 500 to 1,700 rupees per piece	Persia, Turkey, Turkistan, Afghanistan
Islimi	——	From 250 to 400 rupees per piece	Kashmir, Turkistan. To Persia for saddlecloths, curtains, and women's use

[5] Here Moorcroft adds: '. . . and so on to five upwards. In the latter case, however, the cones are somewhat small.'

TRADE NAME	REMARKS	MANUFAC-TURER'S PRICE	MARKETS
Maramat	——	From 150 to 300 rupees per piece	Kashmir, Afghanistan, Persia
Khutherast (*Khatārāst?*)	——	From 150 to 750 rupees a piece	Kashmir, Persia, Afghanistan, Turkistan
Marpih	——	From 200 to 350 rupees a piece	Kashmir, Persia, Afghanistan, Turkistan
Qalam-kār	——	From 300 to 1,000 rupees a piece	Bokhara, Russia, Con-stantinople (but not large)
Tāk-i-angūr	——	From 300 to 500 rupees a piece	Deccan, few to Turkistan
Chap-o-rast	——	From 300 to 700 rupees a piece	Afghanistan, Persia, Baghdad
Do-gul	——	From 500 to 1,000 rupees a piece	Persia, Con-stantinople, Baghdad
Burghabad	——	From 250 to 400 rupees a piece	Kashmir, a little in Hindu-stan, much in Persia and Afghanistan
Gulasaut	——	From 200 to 900 rupees a piece	Afghanistan, Persia
Dawāzda-khat	——	From 200 to 900 rupees a piece	Turkistan, Turkey, Persia

TRADE NAME	REMARKS	MANUFAC-TURER'S PRICE	MARKETS
Dawāzda-rang	——	From 800 to 1,400 rupees a piece	Turkey
Goole parwane (*Gul-o-parvāna?*)	——	From 300 to 450 rupees a piece	Yarkand
Kayehamoo (*Ka'i-amau'a?*) *sabz-kār* *safīd*	These are made by the shawl-weaver alone and go largely into Hindustan where they are dyed, the small green flowers being previously tied up in hard small knots so as to be protected from the action of the dye, and are of course when untied each surrounded by a small white field. Small eyes of spots of yellow, red and of other colours are supposed to harmonize with the green flowers and the new ground, and these are added by embroiderers or *chikān-doz*	From 120 to 130 rupees a piece	—
Qasaba or Rūmāl (woman's veil or square shawl)	$1\frac{1}{2}$ to $2\frac{1}{2}$ *gaz* square	—	—
Khat-dār	——	From 300 to 500 rupees a piece	Hindustan
Māramat	——	From 150 to 300 rupees a piece	Afghanistan, Persia, Turkey
Islimi (with 13 other *Jāmawār* patterns)	——	From 150 to 300 rupees a piece	Afghanistan, Turkey, Persia, Turkistan
Chahār-bāgh	——	From 300 to 350 rupees a piece	Turkey, Russia, a few to Hindustan
Do-hāshiya	——	From 100 to 175 rupees a piece	Hindustan, a few to Persia

TRADE NAME	REMARKS	MANUFAC-TURER'S PRICE	MARKETS
Chand-dār	——	From 50 to 200 rupees a piece	Kashmir, Afghanistan, Turkistan, few to Persia
Chouthidār	——	From 150 to 400 rupees	Persia, Hindustan, Turkey, Baghdad, Turkistan
Shash chouthidār	——	From 250 to 500 rupees	Persia, Hindustan, few to Turkey
Farangi	——	From 100 to 500 rupees	Exported chiefly to Russia
Tarah-armani	——	From 100 to 250 rupees a piece	Exported chiefly to Armenia, also Turkey
Tarah-rūmāl	——	From 120 to 200 rupees	Exported chiefly to Turkey, a few to Turkistan
Sāda (plain)	——	From 12 to 15 rupees	Kashmir (for domestic use)
Shamlas (girdles for the waist, worn by Asiatics)	These are 8 *gaz* in length and 1½ *gaz* broad, and of various colours and patterns. They vary from 50 to 2,000 rupees in price according to the richness of their work	—	—
Sāda (plain)	——	From 50 to 70 rupees a piece	Kashmir, Kabul, Afghanistan, a few to Turkistan

TRADE NAME	REMARKS	MANUFAC- TURER'S PRICE	MARKETS
Hāshiya-dār	——	From 70 to 200 rupees a piece	Kashmir, Kabul, Afghanistan, a few to Turkistan
Phalā-dār	With two *phalās* and two *hāshiyas* (see Glossary). Grounds of different kinds, as with flowers, lines, sprigs, etc.—viz.:	—	—
Matanbāgh	All flowers	From 500 to 2,000 rupees a piece	Persia
Lahri-dār	Waved like water	From 300 to 1,000 rupees a piece	Persia, Turkey, Baghdad
Khānchā-dār	In trays or plates	From 1,000 to 1,700 rupees a piece	Persia, Turkistan, Turkey, a few to Afghanistan
Māramat	Snaky	From 200 to 1,300 rupees a piece	Persia, a few to Turkey
Rāh-dār	Running between parallel lines	From 300 to 800 rupees a piece	Afghanistan, a few to Turkistan and India
Do-shāla se phalā-dār (shawls with three heads)	This variety contains three *phalās* (see Glossary) instead of two and goes only to Tibet	From 100 to 150 rupees a piece	—
Gospech or Patkā, or Turbans	Length from 8 to 10 *gaz*, breadth 1 *gaz*, and of all colours. One variety has two *phalās*, two *tanjirs*, and two *hāshiyas* (see Glossary). Another variety, *Mandila*, sometimes has a *tanjir* and sometimes not. This is from 8 to 10 *gaz* in length and about 12 *girahs* in breadth	From 150 to 800 rupees / From 45 to 70 rupees	— / —

33

TRADE NAME	REMARKS	MANUFAC-TURER'S PRICE	MARKETS
Khalin pashmīna (shawl carpets)	These are sold per square *gaz* and are made of any size in a single piece	From 20 to 40 rupees per square *gaz*	—
Naqsh or Trousers	Some are with, others without seams. The former are made of two pieces which are sewn together by the *rafūgar*, the latter by the *jarrāb-doz* or stocking-maker	From 200 to 500 rupees a pair	—
Chahārkhāna or Netted cloth	Used by women. Length indefinite, breadth from 14 *girahs*	From 5 to 10 rupees a piece	Persia, Hindustan, a few to Afghanistan, and a few in Kashmir
Gul-badan	Length indefinite, breadth from 14 *girahs* to 1 *gaz*	From 5 to 6 rupees a *gaz*	Persia, Afghanistan, New Shah Jahan
Lungi or Girdles	These differ from *shamlas* by being in narrow check and bordered by lines of different colours. L. 3½ *gaz*, W. 1½ *gaz*	From 50 to 75 rupees a piece	Kashmir, Persia
Takhin or Caps	—	From 8 annas to 4 rupees	Kashmir, few to Kabul and Hindustan
Jarrāb or Short Stockings	Flowered and striped in the *guldār* and *māramat* styles	From 1 to 5 rupees	Kashmir, Hindustan, Kabul, Persia, few to Turkey
Moza Pashmīna or Long Stockings	—	From 5 to 25 rupees a piece	Hindustan, Persia, Turkey, Turkistan, Russia
Sakkabposh (*Sāqibposh?*)	—	From 300 to 1,500 rupees	Persia, Turkey, Arabia

TRADE NAME	REMARKS	MANUFAC-TURER'S PRICE	MARKETS
Darparda or Curtains (for doors or windows)	——	The price the same as Jamawar, sold according to measure	Persia, Turkey, Arabia, Russia
Kajjari asp or Saddle-cloth	——	The price the same as Jamawar, sold according to measure	Persia
Kajjari fil or Elephant's housing	——	The price the same as Jamawar, sold according to measure	Hindustan
Bālāposh or Palangposh (quilts or coverlets)	——	From 300 to 1,000 rupees	Turkistan, Persia, Turkey, Russia, a few to Afghanistan
Galāband or Cravat	——	From 12 to 300 rupees	Hindustan
Pistānband or Neckerchief	——	From 5 to 15 rupees	Kashmir, Afghanistan, Persia, Hindustan
Langota or Waist Belts	——	From 15 to 30 rupees	Persia, Afghanistan, a few to Turkistan
Postīn (cloths left long in the Nap to line pelisses)	——	From 500 to 1,000 rupees	Persia
Pāipech or Leggings	Length 2 *gaz*, breadth 1 *girah*. Of all colours	From 2 to 10 rupees	Kabul, Kandahar, Turkistan, Turkey, Persia

TRADE NAME	REMARKS	MANUFAC- TURER'S PRICE	MARKETS
Izārband or Waist Strings	——	From 1 to 15 rupees each	Persia, Afghanistan
Takīn or Pillow-bier	——	The price the same as Jamawar	Persia, Russia, Turkey, Arabia, Hindustan
Khalīta (bags or purses)	——	From 8 annas to 2 rupees	Kashmir, Kabul
Qabr-posh or Shrouds (for tombs)	——	The price the same as Jamawar	Persia, Arabia, Turkistan
Tāqposh (covers or hangings for recesses, cupboards, etc.)	——	The price the same as Jamawar	Persia

APPENDIX 2

Moorcroft's proposals for the emigration of Kashmiri weavers, spinners and pattern-drawers and their settlement in Britain[1]

1. Excerpt from a letter from Moorcroft to Mr C. T. Metcalfe, the East India Company's Resident at Delhi, written at Amritsar, 21 May 1820 (MSS. Eur. F.38).

'. . . I beg to submit to you in relation to the growing importance of the Shawl Trade in Britain and the obvious advantage of obtaining an early superiority in the manufacture of the article, from the process of picking and cleaning the raw material to that of packing shawls in Bales, which in Britain is ill-conducted, it would not be prudent to invite as many Kashmeerees to proceed to Britain as would be able to go through all the processes employed in this manufacture. The argument of the expense of this measure can only be estimated by a comparison of the merits of Kashmeeree and of English artists, a point not yet wholly adjusted, but the absolute expense will not be great considering the present low wages of the spinners and weavers.

The English borrowed the art of printing Chintz from the artists of this country and now surpass their teachers, and a similar event may reasonably be expected in regard to shawls, if the British manufacturers be sufficiently attentive to their real interests, and not suffer immediate profits by cheapness, to delude them from possessing a paramount and permanent command of the market by superiority of manufacture.

Through a complete set of Kashmeeree Shawl Artists the English manufacturers will *per saltum* seize the advantages of the science and manipulation the experience of centuries has supplied to that branch of manufacture, which, through local circumstances, has been favoured and fostered into a most profitable and most extensive trade, supporting many thousands of individuals, and for rivalry in which several European Nations are now contending. When the English Manufacturers shall have gained the whole Mystery of those Artists who are now confessedly the best performers, let them engraft their own improvements, but let them now start with all 'appliances and means to boot'.

---

[1] Proposals for the emigration of Kashmiri weavers and their settlement under French patronage on the island of Madagascar had been published in 1792 by the Abbé Rochon (*Voyage to Madagascar*), but Moorcroft was apparently unaware of this.

English pride of science may be startled at the supposition that any Oriental Workman can excel English Artisans in manufacturing articles on which English industry has long employed its powers, but such presumption arrests the progress of art, and candour must acknowledge superiority in the material, fabric and temper of some of the Sword blades and Gun barrels of the East: I propose to bring on my return some Gun barrels from Lahor for inspection by British Gunsmiths and which cannot fail to astonish them by their beauty.

Luminously satisfactory and abundant as in latter years have been the reasonings and deductions on colours and on mordants and expeditious and cheap, the modes of extracting and applying colouring matters, it will perhaps be found that industry and long practice, stimulated by the desire of gain, have attained a progress in the art of dyeing woollens *permanently* in Kashmeer, that may not yield in general result, to the lucubrations and discoveries affected by experimental philosophy applied to the same object in Europe.

I must request the favour of your obtaining the sentiments of Mr Reding on the matter of inviting some Kashmeerees to emigrate, and if they be favourable, that you will bring it under the notice of the Government, as expeditiously as possible, in any shape you may think fit.

Amongst the many thousands of individuals employed in the Shawl trade in Kashmeer, it would probably be no difficult task to induce two or three families in a noiseless way to leave that country, but I submit to you that it would be more proper, as an affair in which the Government take an interest, to ask Runjeet Singh to allow me to do this publicly, in passing through Kashmeer.

A belief that the water of Kashmeer is essential to produce good shawls, and that such is not to be met with elsewhere, will prevent apprehensions of rivalry. If this measure be determined upon a letter under cover to Khooshwant Rau, the newswriter, directing him to forward it to me by Qasid, will reach me. And in such event I must further beg that you will cause it to be accompanied by a letter of Credit or Bill for two thousand rupees to be employed by me in relieving the pecuniary embarrassments of some families in distress, for such will be the fittest subjects for experiment, and for furnishing way expenses.

Pattern drawers will of course be included in the detail of Artists from possessing the peculiar patterns of Kashmeer, which for a time may be preferred in Europe to those of that country.

There is nothing novel in such transplantation of artists. Louis XV procured Workmen in Muslins from India, but through the negligence of his Ministers

38

many of them perished through want. And Catherine II invited great numbers of Artists in the Silk Trade, from Lyons, who had formed a Manufactory of Brocades, that now supplies most of the north-western parts of Asia with this 'Article'.'

2. Excerpt from Moorcroft's notes written in Kashmir, 4 February 1823 (MSS. Eur. D.264, pp. 43–4):

'It might border on extravagance to advocate the employment of the labour of the hand on an occupation advantageously superseded by machinery of the most efficient description for preparing thread suited for most fabrics of cloth. But if it be a fact as reported that machinery cannot furnish your yarn as well adapted for the manufacture of Shawls as that spun by hand in Kashmeer nothing would be more easy than to induce a few Kashmeeree families to proceed to Britain on very light terms of remuneration. Whether the introduction of the mode of spinning yarn for shawl-cloth would afford much occupation to weakly and indigent females in Britain is competently to be appreciated by individuals now in that country, but on such a presumption the art might be readily diffused. An unsuccessful experiment was made many years ago at the suggestion, it is believed, of Dupleix or of Le Comte de Lally to import fabrics of India, for the purpose of establishing a manufacture of Muslins in France. Emigrants suffered much from the climate, and after having experienced in Paris a reception and treatment not exactly corresponding to that they were thought to expect they were furnished with an Asylum in one of the Grecian islands where drawings of the occupations were taken by the late Mr Tresham and are presumed to be in the possession of the Right Hon. Lord Cawdor. Nothing in the climate of Britain is likely to prove unfriendly to the constitution of Kashmeerees, for at this moment in Kashmeer (Feb. 4th) the thermometer out of doors stands at twenty-four degrees.'

GLOSSARY OF TERMS USED IN KASHMIR SHAWL-WEAVING

'Amli, 'amlikar. Needlework shawl. From Persian 'amli, 'worked'.

'Asli tūs. The true Kashmiri name of the best shawl-wool, derived from a Central Asian species of the wild mountain goat, *Capra hircus*.

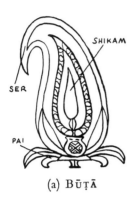

(a) BŪṬĀ

Būṭā. Generic term for the cone, meaning literally 'flower' (see fig. a).

Daur. The running ornament sometimes enveloping the field of a shawl on the inside of the hāshiya and tanjir.

Do-shāla. A pair of shawls.

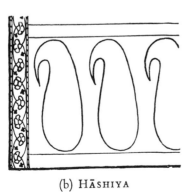

(b) HĀSHIYA

Hāshiya. The narrow-patterned border running down the sides of a shawl (see fig. b).

(c) JHĀL

Jhāl. The decoration which sometimes fills the ground between the cones in the heads of a shawl (see fig. c). It means literally 'net'.

Kanikar. Loom-woven shawl. See also *Tilikar*.

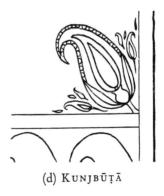

(d) KUNJBŪṬĀ

Kunjbūṭā. Corner ornament (usually a cone) sometimes found in each corner of the field (see fig. d).

Kārkhānadār. The owner of a shawl manufactory.

Kasawa, or Kasaba. A square shawl. See also *Rūmāl*.

Lungi. A girdle. See also *Shamla*.

41

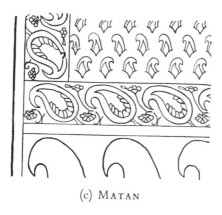

(e) MATAN

Matan. The main field of a shawl (see fig. e).
Mohkun. Shawl-broker.
Naqqāsh. Pattern-drawer.
Pāi. The foot or pediment of a cone (see fig. a).
Pashmīna. The name applied in the West to true Kashmiri shawl-cloth. From Persian *pashm*, 'wool'.

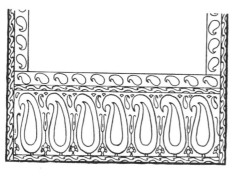

(f) PHALĀ

Phalā. The large-patterned border at each end, or head, of a shawl (see fig. f).

Phīri. Seconds yarn.
Rafūgar. Embroiderer and darner.
Rūmāl. Square shawl.
Ser. The head or tip of a cone (see fig. a).
Shamla. A girdle. See also *Lungi.*
Shikam. The belly of a cone (see fig. a).
Ta'līm-gurū. Pattern-master, responsible for transcribing the colour-pattern into shorthand.

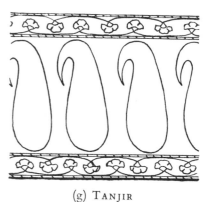

(g) TANJIR

Tanjir. The narrow-patterned border which runs above and below the *phalā*, confining it (see fig. g).
Tarah-gurū. Colour-caller.
Tilikar. Loom-woven shawl. See also *kanikar.*
Tojli. The spool used for threading the coloured weft threads of loom-woven shawls.
Ustād. Master-weaver, applied loosely to all loom-owners, and in the late nineteenth century to overseers at the manufactories.

42

BIBLIOGRAPHY

THE FOLLOWING list of works quoted in the text is not intended as a guide to further reading. For students seeking the latter, a few general comments may be helpful.

For Kashmir shawl history, the most important source is the Moorcroft MSS. written between 1820 and 1823, now preserved at the India Office Library (see under *Manuscripts*). A précis of these manuscripts is included in H. H. Wilson's posthumous compilation, *Travels in the Himalayan Provinces of Hindustan and the Punjab . . . by W. Moorcroft and G. Trebeck*, 2 vols., London, 1841. Wilson's précis, however, which has hitherto been the only source used in quoting Moorcroft on shawl history, is arbitrary and incomplete, and altogether inadequate for the specialist, who must henceforth depend upon the manuscripts.

As far as European shawl history is concerned, J. Rey, *Études pour servir a l'histoire des châles*, Paris, 1823, is of fundamental importance, though concerned primarily with the French industry in its early years. The Edinburgh shawl industry has not hitherto been written about, and very little literature exists on the Norwich shawl, apart from what can be gleaned from the various gazetteers, trade directories, and House of Commons Reports of the early nineteenth century. The Paisley shawl industry, on the other hand, is the subject of several useful monographs. The best and most authoritative is Matthew Blair, *The Paisley Shawl*, Paisley, 1904, which should be read in conjunction with A. M. Stewart, *The history and romance of the Paisley Shawl*, Paisley, 1946. The latter is full of inaccuracies but is nevertheless valuable for its human approach and conveys the spirit of the Paisley weaving tradition better than any other work. Other original but shorter contributions to the subject are W. Cross, *Changes in the style of Paisley Shawls*, Paisley, 1872, which is useful but not always reliable; an anonymous article entitled 'The imitation shawl trade', which appeared in the *Paisley Herald*, 12 November 1859; and another anonymous article, 'Paisley—the shawl trade', which appeared in *Hogg's Weekly Instructor*, Edinburgh, 28 November 1846.

Finally, special mention must be made of the sample books at the Patent Office, London, where many original shawl patterns, with their dates, are registered. Unfortunately, these are not easily accessible, and facilities for study are necessarily dependent upon securing special concessions from the Comptroller-General of Patents.

MANUSCRIPTS AND OTHER ARCHIVAL SOURCE MATERIAL

BRITISH MUSEUM
ANONYMOUS. *The costume of the Persians.* Compiled in the late seventeenth century. Add. MSS. 5254.

CASTLE MUSEUM, NORWICH
Correspondence (in MSS.) exchanged between Norwich residents and Mr Sydney Vacher on the history of the local shawl trade, dated 1897.

INDIA OFFICE LIBRARY AND ARCHIVES (Foreign and Commonwealth Office, London, S.E.1).

ANONYMOUS. *A Journey into Cashmere (in 1846).* Elliot Papers, MSS. Eur. F.58.
EAST INDIA COMPANY. *The Letter Books,* containing copies of despatches from the Directors of the Company to their servants in India and elsewhere.
Home Miscellaneous Volumes, containing original papers exchanged between London and the Company's stations in the East.
MOORCROFT, W. *Notice of particulars respecting the manufacture of shawls in Kashmeer,* dated 25 April 1821. 23 pages. MSS. Eur. D.260.
Shawl manufacture. Dated 1823. 97 pages. MSS. Eur. D.264.
Shawl manufacture. Dated 1823. (A slightly revised version of the preceding MS., addressed to 'The Hon'ble Court of Directors [of the East India Company]'. 49 pages. MSS. Eur. E.113.
Letters to C. T. Metcalfe. Written between 1812 and 1820. MSS. Eur. F.38.
'*Book containing illustrations of the various trades in Kashmir with their respective implements and the corresponding accounts of processes of manufacture.*' MS. volume with 86 original drawings by a native artist, with commentary in Persian. Add. Or. 1660–1745. My earlier assumption (incorporated in the first edition of this book) that the handwriting of the title was Moorcroft's cannot now be sustained. In the opinion of Mrs Mildred Archer, who has catalogued the drawings in this MS. volume for the India Office Library, it is of mid-nineteenth century origin.

PAISLEY MUSEUM AND ART GALLERY
Letters and other papers relating to the evidence given to the Conseil Supérieur du Commerce, Paris, by a delegation of Paisley manufacturers in July 1860.

PATENT OFFICE, LONDON
Sample shawl fabrics, registered in Class viii. Books i to x, dating from 1839 onwards.

CATALOGUES

DELHI EXHIBITION, 1902–3. Official catalogue, entitled *Indian art at Delhi,* compiled by Sir George Watt. Calcutta, 1903.

GREAT EXHIBITION OF 1851. *Illustrated catalogue,* published by the Art Journal, 1851.

MORRISON, McCHLERY & CO., Auctioneers, Glasgow. *Catalogue of Paisley shawls from private collections, sold at the North Gallery, Crown Halls, Glasgow, 2 December 1942. Catalogue of Paisley shawls from private collections, sold at the North Gallery, Crown Halls, Glasgow, 17 February 1943.*

Catalogue of Paisley shawls from private collections, sold at the North Gallery, Crown Halls, Glasgow, 6 December 1943.

PAISLEY FREE PUBLIC LIBRARY AND MUSEUM. *Catalogue of Special Loan Exhibition of Paisley shawls and similar fabrics.* Paisley, 1900.

PARIS UNIVERSAL EXHIBITION OF 1867. *Catalogue of the British Section.* London, 1868.

UNIVERSITY OF LEEDS. *Catalogue of embroidered and woven Indian shawls and historic textiles from the Victoria and Albert Museum. Exhibited in the Department of Textile Industries, 1–15 May 1920.*

GENERAL WORKS

An asterisk marks those works available at the Library of the Victoria and Albert Museum.

*ĀIN-I-AKBARĪ. (The Institutes of Akbar), compiled by Abul Fazl 'Allami. Edited in the original Persian by H. Blochmann, 2 vols. Calcutta, 1872. Trans. in 3 vols. by H. Blochmann and Col. H. S. Jarrett. Calcutta, 1891–94.

*ANONYMOUS. *Kashmeer and its shawls.* London, 1875.

*ANONYMOUS. *New evidence for the study of Kashmir textile history. Journal of Indian Textile History*, no. 1, Ahmedabad, 1955.

ANONYMOUS. *Paisley—the shawl trade. Hogg's Weekly Instructor*, Edinburgh, 28 November 1846, pp. 215–18.

*BADEN POWELL, B. H. *Handbook of the manufactures and arts of the Punjab*, forming vol. ii to the *Handbook of the economic products of the Punjab.* Lahore, 1872.

BAIRD, T. *General view of the County of Middlesex.* Board of Agriculture, London, 1793.

BAKEWELL, R. *Observations on the influence of soil and climate upon wool.* Board of Agriculture, London, 1808.

BARKER, A. F. *The textile industries of Kashmir. Indian Textile Journal*, vol. xliii, no. 508, 1933.

BATES, C. E. *A gazetteer of Kashmir and the adjacent districts.* Calcutta, 1873.

*BERNIER, F. *Travels in the Mogul Empire, 1656–68*, revised trans. by A. Constable. London, 1891.

*BLAIR, M. *The Paisley shawl and the men who produced it.* Paisley, 1904.

*BLAKELY, E. T. *History of the manufactures of Norwich.* Norwich, n.d. (c. 1850).

*BLYTH, G. K. *The Norwich guide.* Norwich, 1842.

BOGLE, G. *Narratives of the Mission of George Bogle to Tibet* (1774), ed. C. R. Markham. London, 1876.

*CHANDRA, M. *Kashmir shawls. Bulletin of the Prince of Wales Museum*, Bombay, no. 3, 1954, pp. 1–24.

CHANDRA, M., and AGRAWALA, V. S. *A note on some cultural references in Srivara Pandita's Rajatarangini. Bulletin of the Prince of Wales Museum*, Bombay, no. 7, 1959–62, pp. 35–40.

*CROSS, W. *Descriptive sketch of changes in the style of Paisley shawls.* The text of a lecture delivered in January 1872, reprinted from *The Paisley and Renfrewshire Gazette.*

Cyclopaedia of India and of Eastern and Southern Asia, ed. E. Balfour, 2nd ed., 5 vols. Madras, 1871.

*DANA, J. C. *Persian textiles.* New Jersey, 1919. Despite its title, this book illustrates chiefly Kashmir and Paisley shawls.

*DUBEUX, L. *La Perse.* Paris, 1841.

*FALKE, O. VON. *Decorative silks.* 1936, fig. 35.

FICHEL, M. *Un mot sur les cachemires des Indes et le cachemire français.* Privately printed. Paris, 1834.

*FISCHEL, O., and BOEHN, M. VON. *Modes and manners of the nineteenth century*, trans. from the German, 4 vols. London, 1927.

FOOT, J. *Life of Hunter.* London, 1794.

*FORBES WATSON, J. *The textile manufactures and the costumes of the people of India.* London, 1867.

FORSTER, G. *Journey from Bengal to England.* 2 vols. London, 1798.

FRYER, J. *A new account of the East Indies and Persia*, 3 vols. Hakluyt Society, 1909–16.

General History of the County of Norfolk. Printed by John Stacey. Norwich, 1829.

GILMOUR, D. *Gordon's Loan sixty-odd years ago.* Privately printed. Paisley, 1891.

*GRAND-CARTERET, J. *Les élégances de la toilette.* Paris, 1911.

GRIER, S. C. *Letters of Warren Hastings to his wife.* London, 1905.

Household Words. A weekly journal, edited by Charles Dickens. London, 1850–59.

HÜGEL, BARON C. *Travels in Kashmir and the Punjab.* London, 1845.

Illustrated catalogue of the Great Exhibition, 1851. Published by the Art Journal, London.

JACQUEMONT, V. *Voyage dans L'Inde*, 4 vols. Paris, 1841.

JOHNSTONE, D. C. *The woollen manufactures of the Punjab.* Lahore, 1885.

JONES, SIR W. *Life, writings and correspondence of Sir William Jones* (ed. by Lord Teignmouth). London, 1807.

*KARPINSKI, C. *Kashmir to Paisley. Bulletin of the Metropolitan Museum*, New York, November 1963, pp. 116–24.

*KING, M. R. *Cashmere shawls. Cincinnati Museum Review*, no. 5, 1921.

LAWRENCE, W. R. *The valley of Kashmir*. London, 1895.

LEGOUX DE FLAIX. *Essai historique, géographique et politique sur l'Indoustan*, 2 vols. Paris, 1807.

*LOMULLER, L. *Existe-t-il des châles Ternaux dessinés par Isabey? Beaux Arts*, no. 120, Paris, 15 April 1949.

McCULLOCH, J. R. *A statistical account of the British Empire*, 2nd ed., 2 vols. London, 1839.

Magazine of Art. London, 1878–1904.

MANRIQUE, S. *The travels of Sebastien Manrique, 1629–43*. Hakluyt Society, 2 vols. 1926–27.

*MANUCCI, N. *Storia do Mogor or Mogul India, 1653–1708*. Trans. by W. Irvine, 4 vols. London, 1906.

*MAZE-SENCIER, A. *Les fournisseurs de Napoléon Iier et des deux Impératrices*. Paris, 1893.

Memorial of the operative weavers in Paisley to the Sheriff Depute of Refrewshire, presented 12 December 1812. (A copy is preserved in Paisley Public Library.)

MERRIMAN, J. J. *John Hunter at Earl's Court, 1764–93*. Privately printed. London, 1886.

MOORCROFT, W. (and Trebeck, G.). *Travels in the Himalayan Provinces of Hindustan and the Punjab; in Ladakh and Kashmir; in Peshawar, Kabul, Kunduz and Bokhara from 1819 to 1825*. (Prepared for the press from original journals and correspondence by H. H. Wilson. 2 vols. London, 1841. This compilation is not an accurate record of Moorcroft's unpublished mss.—for which, see under MANUSCRIPTS.

*MOSSMAN, R. G. *Design techniques of Kashmir handloom textiles. Bulletin of the Needle and Bobbin Club*, vol. 50, New York, 1967, pp. 31–65.

*MURPHY, J. *A treatise on the art of weaving*, 2nd ed. (revised and enlarged). Glasgow, 1827.

New Statistical Account of Scotland, 15 vols., 1845 (the chapter on Paisley was written in 1837).

*PELSAERT, F. *Remonstrantie*, trans. W. H. Moreland and P. Geyl as *Jahangir's India*. London, 1925.

*RACINET, A. *Le costume historique*, 6 vols. Paris, 1888.

RÉMUSAT, MADAME DE. *Memoirs*, trans. Mrs Cashel Hoey and Mr J. Lillic. London, 1880.

Reports from Assistant Handloom Weaver's Commissioners, 1839–40. Printed by order of the House of Commons, in 3 vols (5 parts), 1939–1940.

*REY, J. *Études pour servir à l'histoire des Châles*. Paris, 1823.

*ROCK, C. H. *Paisley shawls: a chapter of the Industrial Revolution*. Paisley Museum and Art Galleries, 1966.

ROE, SIR T. *The embassy of Sir Thomas Roe to the Court of the Great Mogul, 1615–19*, ed. W. Foster. Hakluyt Society, 1899.

*ROSENBLUM, R. *Ingres*. London, 1967.

*RUDD, W. R. *Norwich master weavers. Proceedings of the Norwich Science Gossip Club*, 1911–12.

*SIMPSON, W. *India, ancient and modern: a series of illustrations of the country and people . . . Executed in chromolithographs from drawings by W. S., with descriptive literature by John William Kaye*. London, 1867.

SOUTHEY, T. *The rise, progress and present state of Colonial wools*. London, 1848.

Statistical account of Scotland: from communications of ministers of the different parishes, compiled by Sir John Sinclair, 21 vols. 1791–99.

STEINBACH, LT.-COL. *The Punjab*. London, 1845.

*STEWART, A. M. *The history and romance of the Paisley Shawl*. Paisley, 1946.

TESSIER, M. *Mémoire sur l'importation en France des chevres à duvet de Cachemire*. A reprint of a paper read at L'Académie Royale des Sciences (Paris), 13 September 1819.

THÉVENOT, J. DE. *Troisième partie des voyages de, contenant la relation de l'Hindostan, des nouveaux Mogols, et des autres peuples et pays des Indes*. Paris, 1684.

THORNTON, E. *A gazetteer of the countries adjacent to India*, 2 vols. London, 1844.

46

THORP, R. *Cashmere misgovernment*. London, 1870.

TORRENS, LT.-COL. *Travels in Ladak, Tartary, and Kashmir*. London, 1863.

*TURNER, CAPTAIN S. *An account of an embassy to the court of the Teshoo Lama, in Tibet* (1783). London, 1800.

VALLE, P. DELLA. *The travels of Pietro della Valle*, 2 vols. Hakluyt Society, 1891.

VIGNE, G. T. *Travels in Kashmir*. London, 1842.

*WARNER, SIR F. *The silk industry of the United Kingdom: its origin and development*. London, 1921.

*WATT, SIR G. *Indian art at Delhi, being the official catalogue of the Delhi exhibition, 1902–3*. Calcutta, 1903.

*WEIBEL, A. C. *Two thousand years of textiles*. Detroit Institute of Arts, Detroit, 1952.

WHYTE, D. *The Paisley shawl. Scottish Woollens*, no. 39, June 1949 (4 pp., 7 pls., some in col.).

WHYTE, D. and SWAIN, M. *Edinburgh shawls*. Book of the Old Edinburgh Club, 31st vol., 1962.

*WHYTE, D. *Paisley shawls and others. Costume* (Journal of the Costume Society), no. 4, 1970, pp. 32–6.

WILSON, H. H. Compiler and editor of Moorcroft's posthumous *Travels* (s. v. Moorcroft, William).

WILSON, J. *General view of the agriculture of Renfrewshire*. Board of Agriculture, London, 1812.

CATALOGUE

WHEREVER possible colours have been identified from the first edition of the *British Colour Council dictionary of colour standards* (published in 1934 by the British Colour Council, 13 Portman Square, London, W.1), and the actual chart numbers have been quoted. These identifications relate to the condition of the material when examined, no allowances having been made for dirtiness or fading.

The analyses of fabrics were made by Mr R. J. Varney, formerly Assistant in the Indian Section, Victoria and Albert Museum, who was also responsible for other help in connection with the preparation of the catalogue. Where doubt was felt about analyses, samples were sent to the Director of the Shirley Institute, Manchester, for independent opinion.

FRONTISPIECE. FRAGMENT OF SHAWL-CLOTH: loom-woven, Kashmir, 18th century.
Warp and weft: goat-fleece.
Weave: 2×2 twill, with 88 warps to the inch.
Size: H. 1 ft 10 in. W. 8½ in.
Collection: Calico Museum of Textiles, Ahmedabad. Inv. No. C.14–S.14.

PLATE 1. FRAGMENT OF SHAWL BORDER: loom-woven, Kashmir, 17th century.
Warp and weft: goat-fleece.
Weave: 2×2 twill, with 96 warps to the inch.
Size: W. 14½ in. H. 5¾ in.
Colours: mistletoe, victrix blue, sky green, (dark) beryl blue, cherry, on a banana ground. B.C.C. Nos. 9, 47, 101, 117, 185 and 64.
Collection: Victoria and Albert Museum (given by Miss Gira Sarabhai in 1954). Inv. No. I.S. 70–1954, Neg. No. G.B. 1964.
Remarks: This fragment is probably part of the shawl illustrated in the catalogue of the *Loan exhibition of antiquities*, Coronation Durbar, Delhi, 1911, p. 35, pl. xv (d). There it is described as having been 'conferred as a *khil'at* by one of the late Moghul Emperors on a Chief of Bikaner'. Another, larger fragment of the same shawl is in the Calico Museum of Textiles, Ahmedabad.

PLATE 2. SHAWL FRAGMENT: loom-woven, Kashmir, early 18th century.
Warp and weft: goat-fleece.
Weave: 2×2 twill, with 92 warps to the inch.
Size: H. 11 in. W. 4½ in. Height of flora motif, 7¾ in.
Colours: maize, cyclamen, pink, neyron rose, claret, victrix blue, straw, Cambridge blue, powder blue, and white, on a banana ground. B.C.C. Nos. 5, 33, 35, 36, 47, 51, 191, 193, 1, and 64.
Collection: Victoria and Albert Museum (given by Mr N. H. Heeramaneck in 1924). Inv. No. I.M.48–1924, Neg. No. G.587.

PLATE 3. PART OF A SHAWL: loom-woven, Kashmir, first half of the 18th century.
Warp and weft: goat-fleece.
Weave: 2×2 twill, with 68 warps to the inch.
Size: W. 3 ft 9 in. H. 9½ in. Height of cones, 8 in.
Colours: lichen green, malmaison rose, claret, saxe blue, victrix blue, satinwood, beryl blue, on a maize ground. B.C.C. Nos. 8, 16, 36, 45, 47, 65, 117, and 5.
Collection: Victoria and Albert Museum (bought in 1913). Inv. No. I.M.166–1913. Neg. No. G.586.

PLATE 4. TWO SHAWL FRAGMENTS: loom-woven, Kashmir, late 17th or early 18th century.
Warp and weft: goat-fleece.
Weave: 2×2 twill, the upper fragment with 112 warps to the inch, the lower with 95.
Size: the upper fragment: L. 8 in. W. 5¾ in.; the lower fragment: L. 8 in. W. 7 in.
Colours: the upper fragment: peony red, verdigris, cinnamon on a vanilla ground. B.C.C. Nos. 37, 202, 204, 141;
the lower fragment: straw, saxe blue, green muscat, claret, mole, on a saffron ground. BCC. Nos. 51, 45, 76, 36, 83, 54.
Collection: Victoria and Albert Museum (given by H.M. the Queen), Inv. Nos. I.S.14–1972 (the upper fragment) and I.S.13–1972 (the lower fragment).
Note: From a collection of textile fragments (Inv. Nos. I.S.6–1972 to I.S.33–1972) taken from the many quilted interlinings of a jacket, part of the *Rich War Dress* of Tipu Sahib, Sultan of Mysore. This jacket was amongst the trophies of Seringapatam presented to the Crown by Lord Wellesley in 1799. Samples were removed during recent conservation of the jacket. The bulk of them consisted of *pashmina* fragments from Kashmir shawls.

PLATES 5 and 6. SHAWL: loom-woven, Kashmir, late 17th or early 18th century.
Warp and weft: goat-fleece.
Weave: 2×2 twill, with 116–120 warps to the inch.
Size: L. 6 ft 10 in. W. 4 ft 2 in. Height of cones, 5 in. approx.
Colours: red, yellow, three shades of green, on a cream ground.
Collection: Museum of Fine Arts, Boston, Mass., Inv. No. 45.540.

PLATE 7. SHAWL: loom-woven, Kashmir, late 17th or early 18th century.
Warp and weft: goat-fleece.
Weave: 2×2 twill, with 114 warps to the inch.
Size: L. 9 ft 1 in. W. 2 ft 4 in.
Colours: bottle green, old rose, claret, straw, white and metallic gold, on a green muscat ground.

Collection: Victoria and Albert Museum (bought in 1967). Inv. No. I.S.23–1967, Neg. No. G.A.3386.
Note: The border decoration of florets is outlined in gold-leaf.
Formerly in the Jaipur Palace collection.

PLATE 8. SHAWL FRAGMENT: loom-woven, Kashmir, mid-18th century.
Warp and weft: goat-fleece.
Weave: 2×2 twill, with 94 warps to the inch.
Size: H. 12 in. W. 8½ in. Height of cones, 8¾ in.
Colours: blossom pink, claret, straw, midnight, Cambridge blue, juniper, on a banana ground. B.C.C. Nos. 34, 36, 51, 90, 191, 192, and 64.
Collection: Victoria and Albert Museum (bought in 1913). Inv. No. I.M.169–1913, Neg. No. G.587.

PLATE 9. PART OF A SHAWL: loom-woven, Kashmir, first half of the 18th century.
Warp and weft: goat-fleece.
Weave: 2×2 twill, with 88 warps to the inch.
Size: W. 2 ft H. 9¾ in. Height of cones 7¾ in.
Colours: champagne, blossom pink, peony red, saxe blue, victrix blue, beryl blue, on a cream ground. B.C.C. Nos. 4, 34, 37, 45, 47, 117, and 3.
Collection: Victoria and Albert Museum (bought in 1913). Inv. No. I.M.165–1913, Neg. No. G.587.

PLATE 10. PART OF A SHAWL: loom-woven, Kashmir, second half of the 18th century.
Warp and weft: goat-fleece.
Weave: 2×2 twill, with 94 warps to the inch.
Size: W. 3 ft 11½ in. H. 11 in. Height of cones, 7¼ in.
Colours: champagne, maize, cyclamen pink, claret, forget-me-not, midnight, beryl blue, delphinium, on a cream ground. B.C.C. Nos. 4, 5, 33, 36, 84, 90, 117, 195, and 3.
Collection: Victoria and Albert Museum (bought in 1913). Inv. No. I.M.302–1913, Neg. No. G.589.

PLATE 11. PART OF A SHAWL: loom-woven, Kashmir, second half of the 18th century.
Warp and weft: goat-fleece.

Weave: 2×2 twill, with 72 warps to the inch.
Size: L. 9 ft 4 in. W. 4 ft 4 in. Height of cones, 8 in.
Colours: cyclamen pink, claret, victrix blue, banana, satinwood, delphinium, on a white ground. B.C.C. Nos. 33, 36, 47, 64, 65, 195, and 1.
Collection: Victoria and Albert Museum (given by Miss M. Davis in 1915). Inv. No. I.M.17-1915, Neg. No. G.588.

PLATE 12. SHAWL: loom-woven, Kashmir, *c.* 1770.
Warp and weft: goat-fleece. See Chapter I, Note 19.
Weave: 2×1 twill, with approximately 100 warps to the inch.
Size: L. 6 ft 3¾ in. W. 4 ft 4½ in.
Colours: R.A.F. blue grey, eau-de-nil and white, on a cream ground. B.C.C. Nos. 156, 21, 1 and 3.
Collection: Victoria and Albert Museum (given by Mrs V. Eley and Mrs G. L. Warren in 1958). Inv. No. T.89-1958, Neg. No. GB.1381.
Note: A note from the donors' family states: *Brought from Bengal about 1770 by my maternal grandfather, Thomas Coulson. He was the resident at Copenbazaar in Dacca, Bengal. August 25th, 1907. John Edmund Coulson.*

PLATE 13. SHAWL FRAGMENT: loom-woven, Kashmir, 18th century.
Warp and weft: goat-fleece.
Weave: 2×2 twill, with 93 warps to the inch.
Size: L. 2 ft 3¼ in. W. 2 ft 1½ in.
Colours: almond green, maize, indigo, claret and gault grey, on a cream ground. B.C.C. Nos. 10, 5, 48, 36, 71 and 3.
Collection: Victoria and Albert Museum (given by Mrs Joan V. Winter in 1969). Inv. No. I.S.4-1969, Neg. Nos. GA.3388-9.
Note: formerly in the Hyderabad (Deccan) Palace Collection.

PLATE 14. PART OF A SHAWL: loom-woven, Kashmir, second half of the 18th century.
Warp and weft: goat-fleece.
Weave: 2×2 twill, with 96 warps to the inch.

Size: W. 2 ft 3 in. H. 1 ft 2 in. Height of cones 11½ in.
Colours: neyron rose, claret, victrix blue, banana, falcon, calamine blue, on a pale khaki ground. B.C.C. Nos. 35, 36, 47, 64, 130, 163, and 72.
Collection: Victoria and Albert Museum (bought in 1913). Inv. No. I.M.164-1913, Neg. No. G.591.

PLATE 15. SHAWL: loom-woven, Kashmir, first half of the 19th century.
Warp and weft: goat-fleece.
Weave: 2×2 twill, with 86 warps to the inch.
Size: L. 5 ft 1¼ in. W. 5 ft.
Colours: pastel yellow, claret, calamine blue, R.A.F. blue grey, cream. B.C.C. Nos. 232, 36, 163, 156, 3.
Collection: Victoria and Albert Museum (given by Miss Kathleen Whitehead in 1968). Inv. No. I.S.5-1968, Neg. No. GA.3387.
Note: Like pls. 18 and 19, an example of the type known as a *chand-dār* or *moon-shawl.*

PLATE 16. PART OF A SHAWL: loom-woven, Kashmir, late 18th or early 19th century.
Warp and weft: goat-fleece.
Weave: 2×2 twill, with 54 warps to the inch.
Size: L. 2 ft 6 in. W. 1 ft 9 in.
Colours: red, pink, yellow, green, a shade of blue, on a blue ground.
Collection: Museum of Fine Arts, Boston, Mass. Inv. No. 99, 163, Neg. No. 1732.

PLATE 17. SHAWL: loom-woven, Kashmir, late 18th or early 19th century.
Warp and weft: goat-fleece.
Weave: 2×2 twill, with 76 warps to the inch.
Size: L. 9 ft 7 in. W. 2 ft 7 in.
Colours: warps are a dull green-blue; weft colours form varicoloured square backgrounds for flowers. Three reds, two pinks, three oranges, three yellows, five shades of green, two shades of green-blue, four blues, a violet and a cream.
Collection: Museum of Fine Arts, Boston, Mass. Inv. No. 00.582.

PLATES 18 and 19. SHAWL: loom-woven, Kashmir, early 19th century.
Warp and weft: goat-fleece.
Weave: 2×2 twill, with 66 warps to the inch on the centre piece, and 130 warps to the inch on applied border.
Size: 5 ft 11 in. by 5 ft 11 in.
Colours: red, pink, three blues, green, yellow, on a cream ground.
Collection: Museum of Fine Arts, Boston, Mass. Inv. No. 21.1333, Neg. No. 14679.

PLATE 20. SHAWL: loom-woven, Kashmir, *c.* 1800.
Warp and weft: goat-fleece.
Weave: 2×2 twill, with 100 and 80 warps to the inch.
Size: L. 13 ft 4 in. W. 4 ft 7 in. Height of floral motif, $11\frac{1}{2}$ in.
Colours: Main ground, Brunswick green.

Wide border, victrix blue, coral, bunting yellow, raspberry, white, on a bunting azure ground.

Narrow border, victrix blue, Brunswick green, bunting yellow, raspberry, on a white ground. B.C.C. Nos. M.grd., 104. W.brdr., 47, 93, 113, 116, 159, 1, and 131. N.brdr., 47, 104, 113, 159, and 1.
Collection: Calico Museum of Textiles, Ahmedabad. Ref. No. 276.

PLATE 21. SHAWL: loom-woven, Kashmir, *c.* 1800.
Warp and weft: goat-fleece.
Weave: 2×2 twill, with 90 warps to the inch.
Size: L. 10 ft 5 in. W. 4 ft 6 in.
Colours: cyclamen pink, peony red, victrix blue, saffron, stone white, cedar green, delphinium, on a moss green ground. B.C.C. Nos. 33, 37, 47, 54, 61, 80, 195 and 174.
Collection: Property of the Countess of Powis.
Remarks: This shawl is claimed on hearsay evidence to have been brought from India by the 2nd Lord Clive, about 1804.

PLATE 22. SCARF OR GIRDLE: loom-woven, Kashmir, early 19th century.
Warp and weft: goat-fleece (the edgings reinforced with silk warps).

Weave: 2×2 twill, with 96 warps to the inch. End borders separately woven.
Size: L. 9 ft 4 in. W. 1 ft 1 in.
Colours: maize, mistletoe, malmaison rose, claret, victrix blue, bunting azure, on a cream ground. B.C.C. Nos. 5, 9, 16, 36, 47, 131, and 3.
Collection: Victoria and Albert Museum (given by the National Art Collections Fund in 1950). Inv. No. I.S.177–1950, Neg. No. M.285.

PLATE 23. PART OF A SHAWL: loom-woven, Kashmir, early 19th century.
Warp and weft: goat-fleece.
Weave: 2×2 twill, with 90 warps to the inch.
Size: L. 4 ft 1 in. W. 1 ft 3 in.
Colours: A ground pattern of claret, saxe blue, straw, geranium pink, juniper, and jet black; plus, in the border, cream, Indian yellow, and cardinal. B.C.C. Nos. 36, 45, 184, 192, 220, plus 3, 6, and 186.
Collection: Royal Scottish Museum, Edinburgh. Inv. No. 1920–393.

PLATE 24. PART OF A SHAWL: loom-woven, Kashmir, *c.* 1820.
Warp and weft: goat-fleece.
Weave: 2×2 twill, with 75 warps to the inch.
Size: L. 2 ft 5 in. W. 1 ft 9 in. Height of large cones, 1 ft 3 in. Depth of lead, 1 ft $3\frac{1}{2}$ in.
Colours: ivory, maize, lichen green, nigger brown, peony red, indigo, forget-me-not, orchid pink, cypress green, beetroot. B.C.C. Nos. 2, 5, 8, 20, 37, 48, 84, 106, 175, 200.
Collection: Victoria and Albert Museum (bought in 1883). Inv. No. 1573–1883 I.S., Neg. No. G.323.

PLATE 25. SHAWL FRAGMENT: loom-woven, Kashmir, *c.* 1820.
Warp and weft: goat-fleece.
Weave: 2×2 twill, with 86 warps to the inch.
Size: L. 1 ft $11\frac{1}{2}$ in. W. 1 ft $8\frac{1}{2}$ in. Height of cones, 1 ft 1 in.
Colours: maize, eau-de-nil, cyclamen pink, peony, indigo, écru, calamine blue, with peony warp threads. B.C.C. Nos. 5, 21, 33, 37, 48, 63, 163, plus 37 (warp threads).
Collection: Victoria and Albert Museum

(bought in 1883). Inv. No. 2090–1883 I.S., Neg. No. G.324.

PLATE 26. SCARF OR GIRDLE: embroidered with the needle, Kashmir, c. 1830.

Worked with silks on a ground of goat-fleece, the latter of 2×2 twill, with 100 warps to the inch. The embroidery in stem, satin and darning stitches.

Size: L. 8 ft 4 in. W. 2 ft 4½ in.

Colours: The centre field is cardinal red (B.C.C. No. 186). The embroidery is blossom pink, victrix blue, satinwood, salmon, bunting azure, nutria, juniper, jet black, and stone white, on a peony red ground. B.C.C. Nos. 34, 47, 65, 91, 131, 139, 192, 220, 61, and 37.

Collection: Victoria and Albert Museum (given by Mrs Marian Lewis in 1907). Inv. No. 501–1907, Neg. No. 57659.

PLATE 27. SCARF OR GIRDLE: loom-woven, Kashmir, embroidered in stem, satin and darning stitches with wool, illustrating stories from Nizami's *Khamsa, c.* 1840.

Warp and weft: goat-fleece.

Weave: 1×1 twill, with 2×2 twill strip at each end. 70 warps to the inch.

Size: L. 4 ft 11 in. W. 1 ft 6 in.

Colours: neyron rose, rose pink, cyclamen pink, beryl blue, bunting azure, cherry, juniper, stone white, on a jet black ground. B.C.C. Nos. 35, 52, 53, 117, 131, 185, 192, 61, and 220.

Collection: Victoria and Albert Museum (transferred from the India Office in 1879). Inv. No. 0803 I.S., Neg. No. 57660.

PLATE 28. GIRDLE OR SCARF: embroidered with the needle, probably worked by Kashmiri emigrant in the Punjab, second half of the 19th century.

Worked with silks on a plain muslin ground of 66 warps to the inch. The embroidery is inlaid oriental stitch and stem stitch.

Size: L. 4 ft 9 in. W. 1 ft. Height of sprays, 5 in.

Colours: maize, almond green, blossom pink, saffron, water green, bunting azure, cherry, jet black, on a stone white ground. B.C.C. Nos. 5, 10, 34, 54, 99, 131, 185, 220 and 61.

Collection: Victoria and Albert Museum (given by Miss M. K. Lawrence in 1920). Ref. No. I.M.212–1920, Neg. No. 57661.

Remarks: This piece has unusual features, including the use of muslin for the ground. The style, however, has points of similarity with other Kashmir shawls of the period (cf. pl. 37, especially the treatment of the cones in the corner of the field).

PLATE 29. PART OF A SHAWL: loom-woven, Kashmir, c. 1820.

Warp and weft: goat-fleece.

Weave: 2×2 twill, with 72 warps to the inch.

Size: L. 2 ft 5½ in. W. 1 ft 7½ in. Height of large cones, 10¾ in. Height of small cones, 4 in.

Colours: mistletoe, peony red, straw, chartreuse yellow (nrst.), midnight, falcon, old rose, sky blue, delphinium, écru on a ruby ground. B.C.C. Nos. 9, 37, 51, 75, 90, 130, 157, 162, 196, 63 and 38.

Collection: Victoria and Albert Museum. No Inv. No., Neg. No. G.595.

PLATE 30. PART OF A SHAWL: loom-woven, Kashmir, c. 1820.

Warp and weft: goat-fleece.

Weave: 2×2 twill, with 64 warps to the inch.

Size: L. 2 ft 2 in. W. 2 ft 2 in. Height of cones, 7 in.

Colours: mistletoe, nigger brown, victrix blue, straw, strawberry pink, larkspur, on a peony red ground. Main ground, claret. B.C.C. Nos. 9, 20, 47, 51, 182, 196 and 37. Main ground, 36.

Collection: Victoria and Albert Museum (bought in 1883). Inv. No. 1359b–1883 I.S., Neg. No. G.598.

PLATE 31. PART OF A SHAWL: loom-woven, Kashmir, c. 1830.

Warp and weft: goat-fleece.

Weave: 2×2 twill, with 72 warps to the inch.

Size: L. 3 ft 6 in. W. 1 ft 7 in. Height of large cones, 11 in.

Colours: champagne, écru, midnight, bunting azure, old rose, raspberry, garnet on a garnet warp; plus, in narrow border, Cambridge blue and delphinium on a cream ground. B.C.C.

Nos. 4, 63, 131, 157, 159, and 160, plus 191, 195, and 3.
Collection: Victoria and Albert Museum (bought in 1883), Inv. No. 2084a–1883, Neg. No. G.320.

PLATE 32. PART OF A SHAWL: loom-woven, Kashmir, *c.* 1825.
Warp and weft: goat-fleece.
Weave: 2 × 2 twill, with 75 warps to the inch.
Size: L. 2 ft 5 in. W. 1 ft 5 in. Height of large cones, 10¼ in. Depth of lead, 10½ in.
Colours: blossom pink, peony red, spectrum blue, turquoise green, apricot, garnet, jet black, on a cream ground. B.C.C. Nos. 34, 37, 86, 121, 143, 160, 220 and 3.
Collection: Victoria and Albert Museum (bought in 1883). Inv. No. 2081a–1883 I.S., Neg. No. M.705.

PLATE 33. PART OF A SHAWL: loom-woven, Kashmir, *c.* 1830.
Warp and weft: goat-fleece.
Weave: 2 × 2 twill, with 94 warps to the inch.
Size: L. 4 ft 4 in. W. 2 ft 6 in.
Colours: nigger brown, claret, peony red, lemon, garnet, cypress green, juniper, delphinium, on a cream ground. B.C.C. Nos. 20, 36, 37, 52, 160, 175, 192, 195 and 3.
Collection: Victoria and Albert Museum (bought in 1883). Inv. No. 1685–1883 I.S., Neg. No. G.321.

PLATE 34. SHAWL: loom-woven, Kashmir, *c.* 1830.
Warp and weft: goat-fleece.
Weave: 2 × 2 twill, with:
84 warps to the inch.
60   „   „   „   „   white ground.
110   „   „   „   „   narrow border.
Size: L. 9 ft 8 in. W. 4 ft 7 in. Height of cones, 1 ft 1½ in.
Colours: cream, Indian yellow, claret, peony red, straw, midnight, old rose, sky blue, Cambridge blue, juniper, delphinium, jet black on a cream *centre* ground. B.C.C. Nos. 3, 6, 36, 37, 51, 90, 157, 162, 191, 192, 195, 220 with 3 (centre ground).
Collection: Victoria and Albert Museum (bought in 1883). Inv. No. 2000–1883 I.S., Neg. No. M.1566. Colour slide No. 46688.

PLATE 35. SHAWL: loom-woven, Kashmir, early 19th century.
Warp and weft: goat-fleece.
Weave: 2 × 2 twill, with 82 warps to the inch.
Size: L. 9 ft 11 in. W. 4 ft 1 in. Five rows of cones, height of each cone, 2⅜ in.
Colours: blossom pink, claret, straw (traces), beryl blue, nutria, geranium pink, delphinium (two shades), jet black (darns), on a champagne ground. B.C.C. Nos. 34, 36, 51, 117, 139, 184, 195, 220 and 4.
Note—In almost every case the brown thread (nutria), has been replaced with black darning.
Collection: Victoria and Albert Museum (bequeathed by Sir Michael Sadler in 1948). Inv. No. I.S.95–1948, Neg. No. M.649.
Remarks: Shawls with designs of this type were made without interruption from the late 18th century until the mid-19th. For an example illustrated in a Rajput miniature dated 1795, see H. Goetz in *Jahrbuch der Asiatische Kunst,* vol. i, pl. 39.

PLATE 36. SHAWL: loom-woven, Kashmir, *c.* 1830.
Warp and weft: goat-fleece.
Weave: 2 × 2 twill, with 86 warps to the inch.
Size: L. 12 ft 3 in. W. 4 ft 2 in. Height of large cones, 10½ in. Height of small cones on ground, 2½ in.
Colours: maize, cyclamen pink, peony red, midnight, beryl blue, delphinium, beetroot, jet black, on a cream ground. B.C.C. Nos. 5, 33, 37, 90, 117, 195, 200, 220 and 3.
Collection: Victoria and Albert Museum (bequeathed by Sir Michael Sadler in 1948). Inv. No. I.S.96–1948, Neg. No. G.322.

PLATE 37. REVERSIBLE SCARF: loom-woven, some pattern-outlines needle embroidered, Kashmir, 1865.
Warp and weft: goat-fleece.
Weave: 2 × 2 twill, with 100 warps to the inch in the main pattern and 92 warps to the inch in the border.
Size: L. 8 ft 4 in. W. 1 ft 5 in.
Colours: malachite green, ruby, saffron, marigold, amaranth pink, beryl blue, garter blue, pansy, cardinal, jet black, cream, on a cream

ground. B.C.C. Nos. 23, 38, 54, 56, 107, 117, 132, 180, 186, 220, and 3.

Collection: Victoria and Albert Museum (transferred from the India Office in 1879). Inv. No. 0804 I.S., Neg. No. M.284.

Note—Attached to this scarf is a label which reads: 'Scarf of quite new fabric. Shows the same on both sides. Locality: Kashmir. Exhibitor: Dewān Kirpa Rām. Price £37 12 0.' Catalogue of the British Section, Paris Univ. Exhibition of 1867. London, 1868. Group iv, Class xxxii, no. 12 (p. 289).

PLATE 38. MAN'S OVERCOAT: made up from Kashmir shawl-cloth, loom-woven, early 19th century.

Warp and weft: goat-fleece.

Weave: 2×2 twill, with 80 warps to the inch.

Size: L. 4 ft. W. (across sleeves) 5 ft 2 in.

Colours: maize, malmaison rose, claret, saxe blue, victrix blue, geranium pink, Cambridge blue, on a cream ground. B.C.C. Nos. 5, 16, 36, 45, 47, 184, 191 and 3.

Collection: Victoria and Albert Museum (bought in 1928). Inv. No. I.M.32–1928, Neg. No. G.1026.

PLATE 39. SHAWL: loom-woven, Kashmir, *c.* 1870.

Warp and weft: goat-fleece.

Weave: 2×2 twill, with 82 warps to the inch.

Size: L. 10 ft 6 in. W. 4 ft 11½ in.

Colours: cream, Indian yellow, malachite green, petunia, peacock blue, jet black, on a Union Jack Red ground. B.C.C. Nos. 3, 6, 23, 108, 120, 220, and 210.

Collection: Property of Mrs MacCormack, 23 Courtfield Gardens, London, S.W.5.

PLATE 40. SHAWL: loom-woven, Kashmir, mid-19th century, backed and used as a curtain.

Warp and weft: goat-fleece.

Weave: 2×2 twill, with 96 warps to the inch.

Size: L. 10 ft 2 in. W. 4 ft 6 in. Height of large cones, 2 ft 3 in.

Colours: (dark) malmaison rose, claret, peony red, ruby, straw, green muscat, sky green, cardinal, jet black, with centre ground écru, pattern warp cardinal and narrow border

banana. B.C.C. Nos. 16, 36, 37, 38, 51, 76, 161, 186, 220 with 63, 168 and 64.

Collection: Victoria and Albert Museum (given by H.H. The Maharaja Bahadur Sir Prodyot Coomar Tagore in 1933). Inv. No. I.M.14–1933, Neg. No. M.283.

PLATE 41. SHAWL: loom-woven and finished-off with the needle, Kashmir, *c.* 1865.

Warp and weft: goat-fleece.

Weave: 2×2 twill, with 84 warps to the inch.

Size: L. 7 ft 4 in. W. 7 ft 2 in.

Colours: guardsman red, old rose, beryl blue, mastic, bunting azure, cossack green, pea green, neyron rose, carrot, maize, violet, ruby, gold, pigeon grey, golden brown, mayflower lilac, almond shell, chilli, green muscat, stone white, and jet black. B.C.C. Nos. 126, 157, 117, 167, 131, 105, 172, 35, 144, 5, 179, 38, 114, 189, 74, 228, 67, 98, 76, 61 and 220.

Collection: Victoria and Albert Museum (bought in 1954). Inv. No. I.S.8–1954, Neg. No. GA.3385.

PLATES 42 TO 44. MAP-SHAWL (*naksha*), wool, embroidered in multi-coloured wools with a pictorial map of Srinagar, Kashmir, third quarter of the 19th century.

The ground consists of rectangles of twill-weave wool, seamed together. On this ground the embroidery has been worked in fine wools, mainly in darn-stitch, satin-stitch and stem-stitch, creating on the surface the effect of a woven design.

An embroidered Persian inscription is set at regular intervals round the border, and further inscriptions are scattered among the buildings.

Size: L. 7 ft 6 in. W. 6 ft 6 in.

Colours: beryl blue, white, honey bird, turquoise blue, bunting azure, bottle green, almond green, golden brown, buff, straw, cardinal, peony red, claret, blossom pink, eau-de-nil, vanilla, olive wood, signal red, old gold, oyster grey, jet black and cream. B.C.C. Nos. 117, 1, 119, 118, 131, 25, 10, 74, 66, 51, 186, 37, 36, 34, 21, 141, 205, 208, 115, 31, 220 and 3.

Collection: Victoria and Albert Museum (given by Mrs Estelle Fuller in 1970). Inv. No. I.S. 31–1970, Neg. Nos. GA.1526 to GA.1530.

INDEX

French influence in Kashmir, 15–16
French shawls, 24–5

Goat, species producing shawl-wool, 4, 21
Goat-fleece, sources of, 4–6, 9, 20–4
Goats, attempts to naturalize in Europe, 21–4
Golconda school of painting, Kashmir shawls depicted in, 11
Grant, Colonel J. A., 3 n.9, 8 n.30, 16 n.56
Grier, S. C., 21 n.9, 45
Gujrat (Punjab), shawl-weaving at, 9
Gulab Singh, Sikh ruler, 9, 24
Gurdaspur, 9

Harness-loom, 20, 24
Hastings, Warren, 21 and n.9, 45
Herodotus, 1 n.2
Himalayan ibex, 5
Himalayan mountain sheep, 4, 21
Household Words, 14, 15 n.51, 45
Hügel, Baron Charles, 1 n.3, 45
Hunter, John, 22, 46
Hussain Qūli Khan shawls (Persia), 18
Hyderabad (Deccan) Palace Collection, shawl formerly in, 51 and pl. 13

Indian Institute, Oxford, 21 n.9
India Office Library, London, 6, 43, 44
Ingres, 15 and n.53

Jacquard loom, 18, 24–5
Jaipur Palace Collection, shawl formerly in, 50 and pl. 7
Jamdanis, or Indian figured cottons, 2
Jayakar, Pupul, 2 n.6
Jones, Sir William, 21–2 and 22 n.13, 46
Joubert, M. Amedéé, 23

Kangra, shawl-weaving at, 9
Kārkhānadārs, or owners of large shawl manu-factories, 8, 41
Karpinski, Caroline, 12 n.46, 46
Kashmir shawls, British imitations of, 19–21;

export figures, 18 n.64; first reach Europe, 13, 19; French imitations of, 24–5; in Mughal period, 1, 5, 6, 10 and n.41, 49; loom-woven (*tilikar*), 2–3, 6–9, 42; needle-worked (*'amli*), 3–4, 10 n.41, 13–14; of patchwork construction, 3
Khwāja Yūsuf, (see under Yūsuf, Khwāja)
Kirghiz tribes, nomadic, of Western Kazakhstan, 23
Kirman Province, Persia, embroiderers from, 4; goat-fleece from, 9, 22 n.14; sheep's wool from, 9

Ladakh, 5, 21, 47
Lahore, 9, 17, 38
Loom-owner (Kashmir), (see *Ustād*)
Louis XV of France, 38
Ludhiana, 9
Lyons, France, 18, 39

MacCormack, Mrs, shawl owned by, 55, and pl. 39
Maharaja Gulab Singh (see Gulab Singh)
Maharaja Ranjit Singh (see Ranjit Singh)
Manrique, Sebastien, 9 n.35, 10 and n.41, 46
Manucci, Niccolao, 5 n.17, 46
Map-shawls (Kashmir), 14 and n.50, and pls. 42–4
Metropolitan Museum of Art, New York, 12 and n.46, and illus. nos. 6–13
Millar and Sons, Paisley shawl-merchants, 23
Mohkuns, or shawl-brokers (Kashmir), 8, 42
'Moon-shawls' (Kashmir), (see *Chand-dār*)
Moorcroft, William, 2 and n.8, 3 n.11, 4 and n.12, 5 n.15 and n.18, 6 and n.21, 8 and n.28, 9, 13 and n.47, 15, 18 n.64, 20 and n.7, 22, 24, 27, 37, 39, 43, 44, 46
Museum of Fine Arts, Boston, 50, 51, 52, and pls. 5, 6, 16, 17, 18 and 19

Naqqāsh, or pattern-drawer (Kashmir), 2, 7 and n.24, 38, 42, and illus. no. 2
Needleworked shawls (see *'Amli*)
Nizami's *Khamsa* ('Five poems'), 14, 53, and pl. 27
Norwich shawls, 19, 20, 43, 44
Nurpur, 9

THE PLATES

PLATE I. Fragment of shawl: loom-woven. Kashmir, *c*. 1680

PLATE 2. Fragment of shawl:
loom-woven, Kashmir, early eighteenth century

PLATE 4. Two fragments of shawl: loom-woven,
Kashmir, late seventeenth or early eighteenth century

PLATE 3. Fragment of shawl: loom-woven,
Kashmir, first half of the eighteenth century

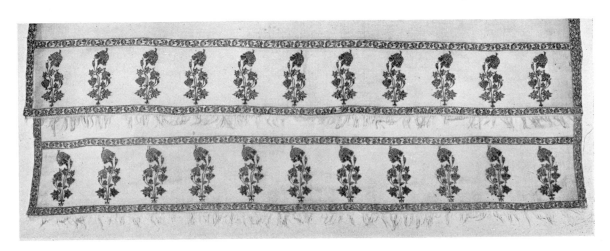

PLATE 5. End-borders of a shawl: loom-woven, Kashmir, early eighteenth century

PLATE 6. Detail of plate 5

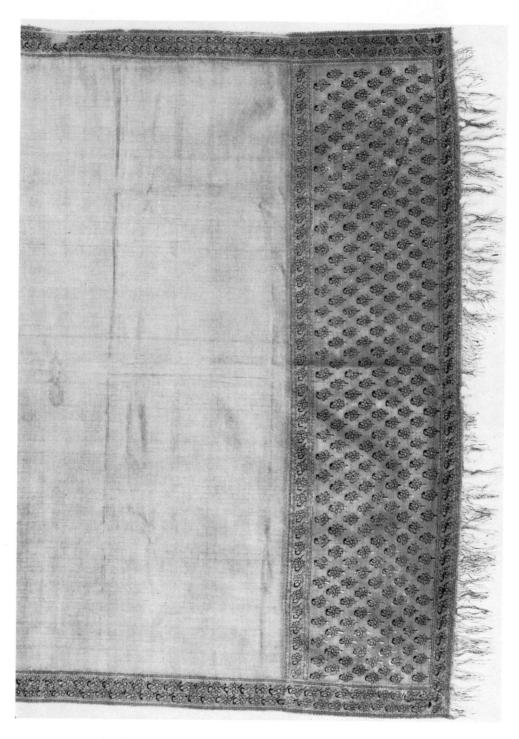

PLATE 7. Detail of shawl: loom-woven, Kashmir, late seventeenth or early eighteenth century

PLATE 8. Fragment of shawl: loom-woven, Kashmir, mid-eighteenth century

PLATE 9. Fragment of shawl: loom-woven, Kashmir, mid-eighteenth century

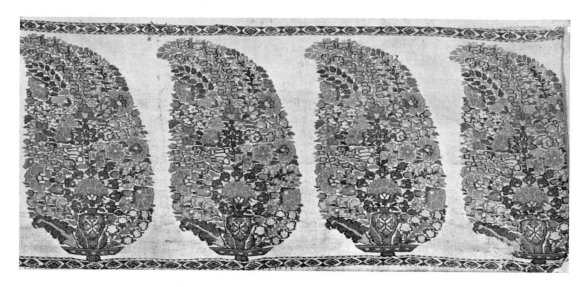

PLATE 10. Fragment of shawl: loom-woven, Kashmir, second half of the eighteenth century

PLATE 11. Detail of a shawl: loom-woven, Kashmir, second half of the eighteenth century

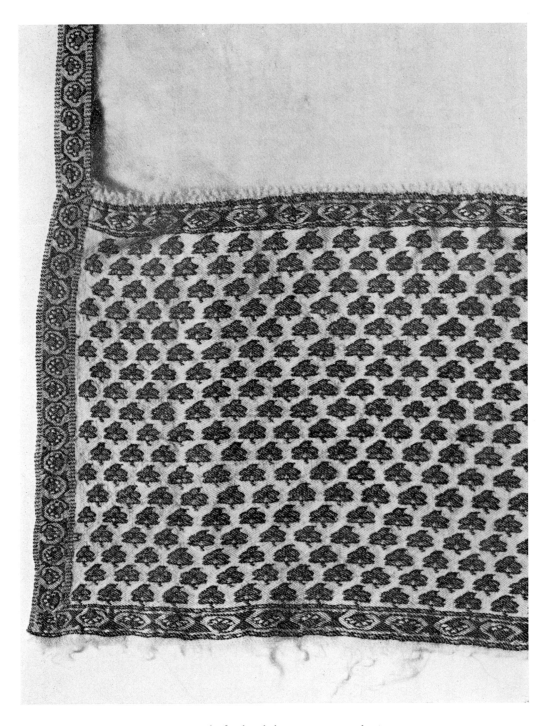

PLATE 12. Detail of a shawl: loom-woven, Kashmir, *c.* 1770

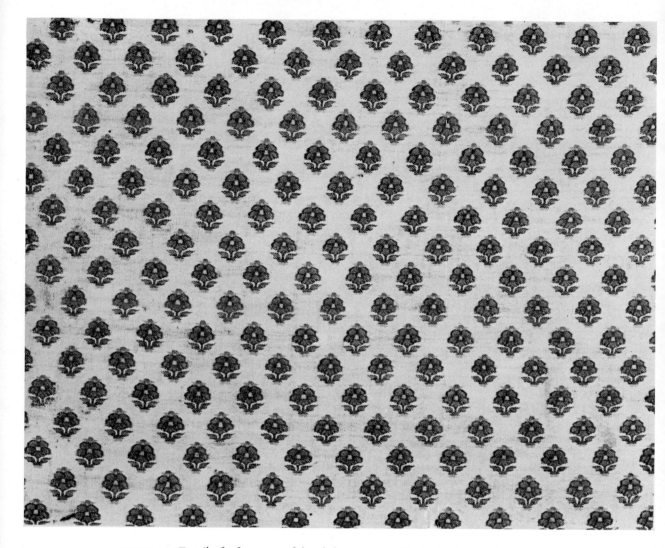

PLATE 13. Detail of a fragment of shawl: loom-woven, Kashmir, eighteenth century

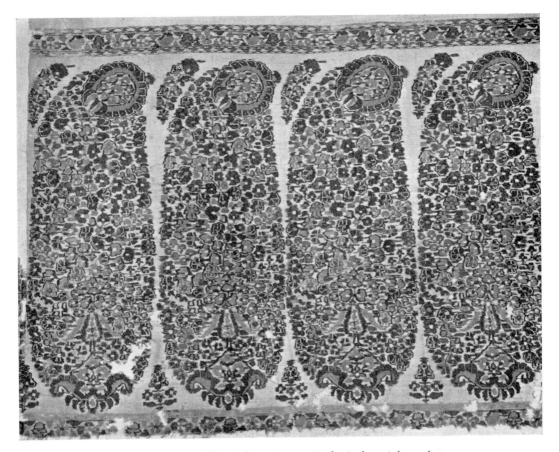

PLATE 14. Fragment of shawl: loom woven, Kashmir, late eighteenth century

PLATE 15. Detail of a shawl: loom-woven, Kashmir, first half of the nineteenth century

PLATE 16. Piece of shawl-cloth: loom-woven, Kashmir, late eigtheenth or early nineteenth century

PLATE 17. Piece of shawl-cloth: loom-woven, Kashmir, late eighteenth or early nineteenth century

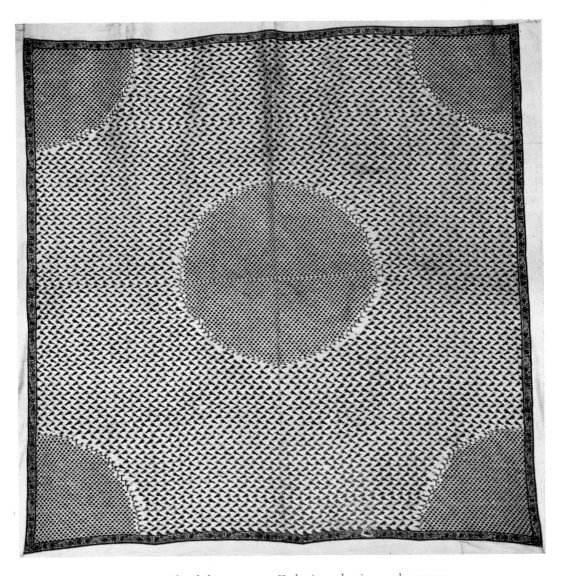

PLATE 18. Shawl: loom-woven, Kashmir, early nineteenth century

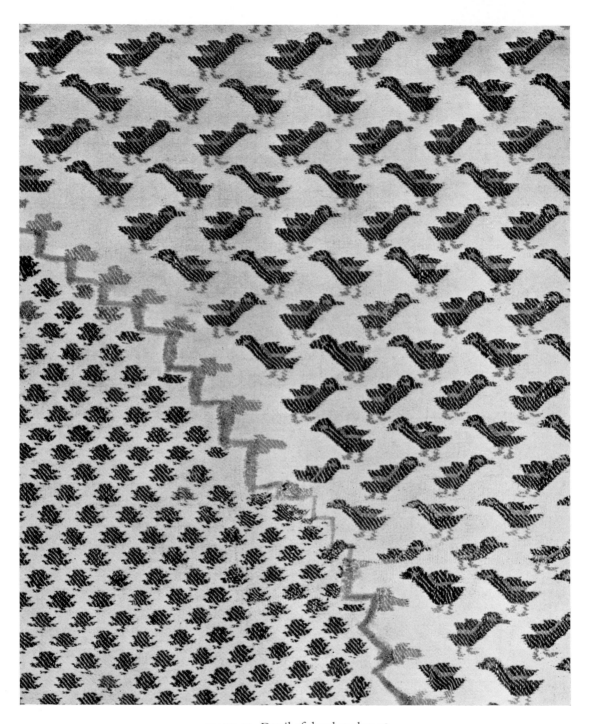

PLATE 19. Detail of shawl at plate 18

PLATE 20. Detail of shawl: loom-woven, Kashmir, *c.* 1800

PLATE 21. Detail of shawl: loom-woven, Kashmir, *c.* 1800

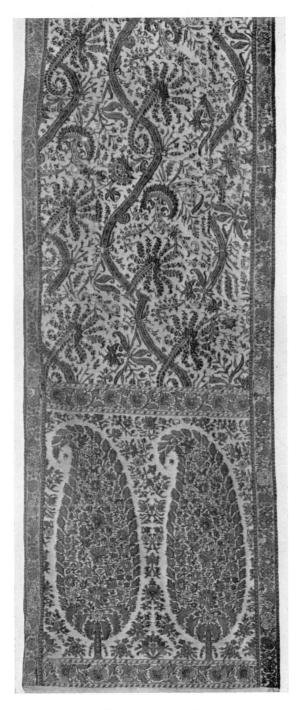

PLATE 22. Girdle: loom-woven, Kashmir, second
quarter of the nineteenth century

PLATE 23. Part of a girdle: loom-woven, Kashmir, late eighteenth or early nineteenth century

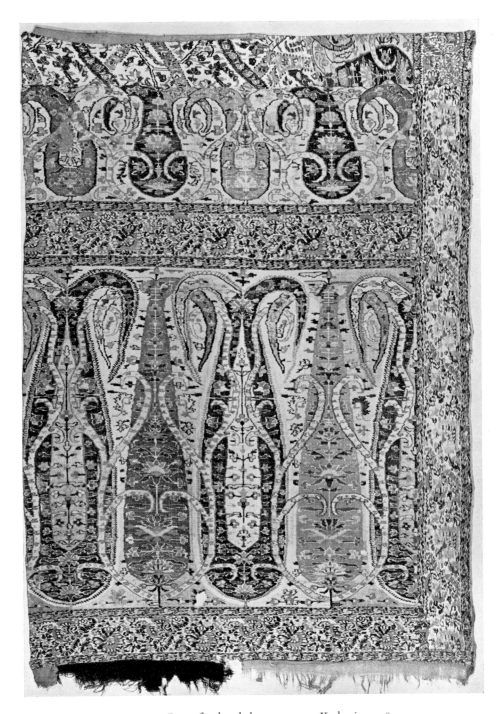

PLATE 24. Part of a shawl: loom-woven, Kashmir, *c.* 1820

PLATE 25. Part of a shawl: loom-woven, Kashmir, *c.* 1820

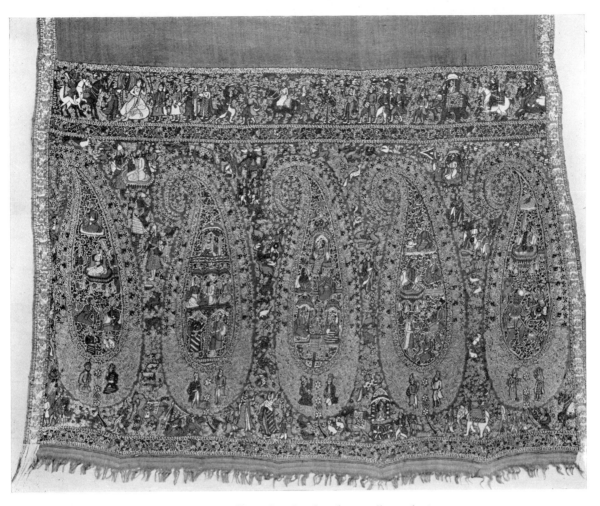

PLATE 26. Scarf or girdle: embroidered with a needle, Kashmir, *c.* 1830

PLATE 27. Scarf or girdle: embroidered with a needle, Kashmir, *c.* 1840

PLATE 28. Scarf or girdle: embroidered with a needle, possibly Punjab, *c.* 1860

PLATE 29. Part of a shawl: loom-woven, Kashmir, *c.* 1820

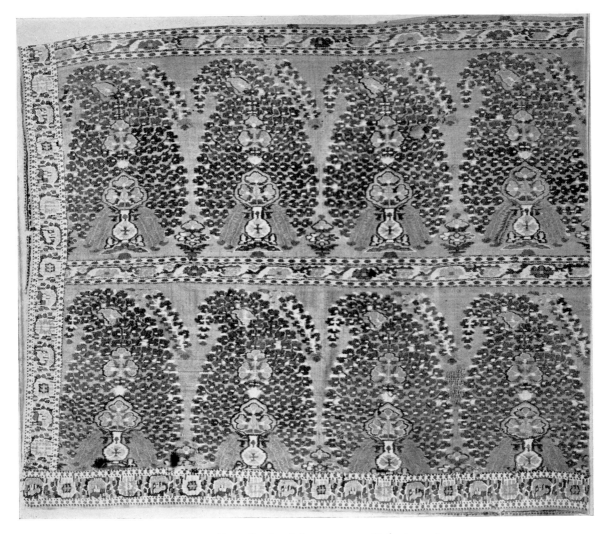

PLATE 30. Part of a shawl: loom-woven, Kashmir, *c.* 1830

PLATE 31. Part of a shawl: loom-woven, Kashmir, *c.* 1830

PLATE 32. Part of a shawl: loom-woven, Kashmir, c. 1825

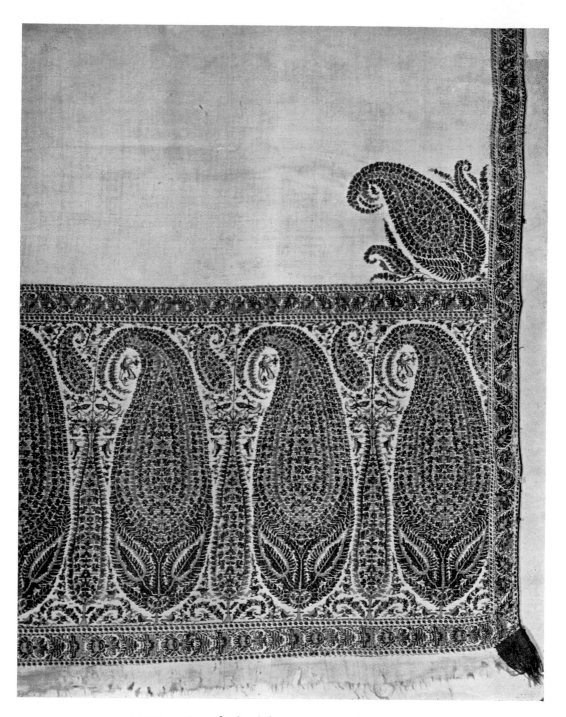

PLATE 33. Part of a shawl: loom-woven, Kashmir, *c.* 1830

PLATE 34. Detail of shawl: loom-woven, Kashmir, c. 1830

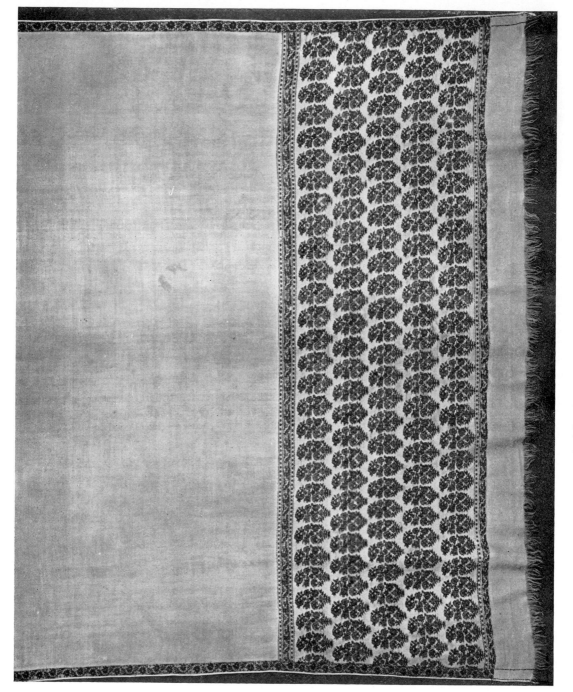

PLATE 35. Detail of shawl: loom-woven, Kashmir, early nineteenth century

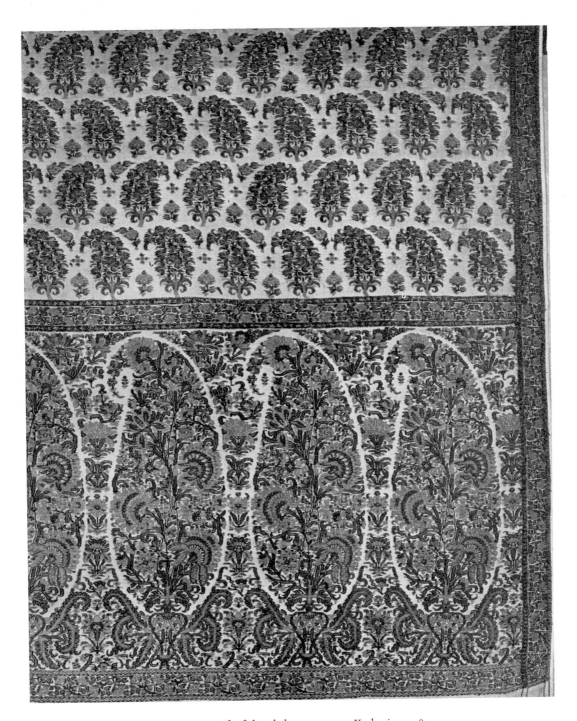

PLATE 36. Detail of shawl: loom-woven, Kashmir, *c.* 1830

PLATE 37. Scarf or girdle: reversible weave, Kashmir, 1865

PLATE 38. Man's coat: loom-woven, Kashmir, early nineteenth century

PLATE 39. Detail of shawl: loom-woven (patchwork construction), Kashmir, *c.* 1870

PLATE 40. Shawl: loom-woven, Kashmir, *c.* 1860

PLATE 41. Detail of shawl: loom-woven and finished-off with the needle, Kashmir, *c.* 1865

PLATE 42. Map-shawl: embroidered with a needle, Kashmir, third quarter of the nineteenth century

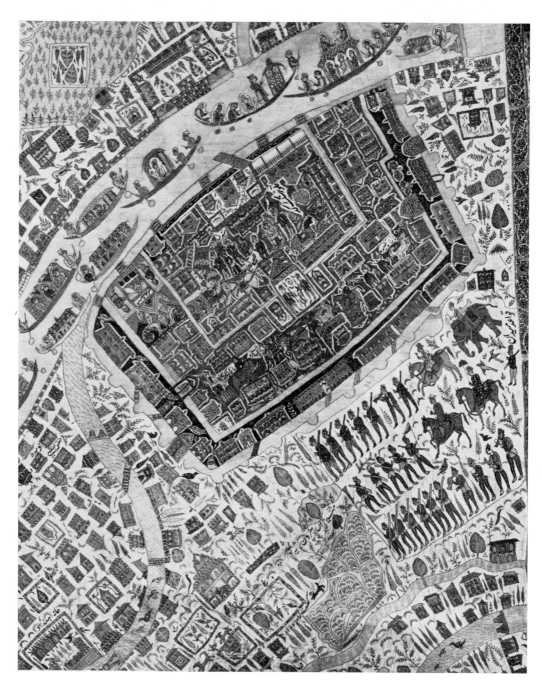

PLATE 43. Detail of plate 42

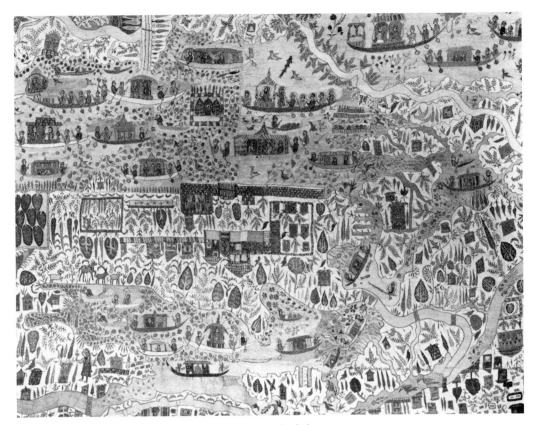

PLATE 44. Detail of plate 42